Windows into the World Church

Christ at work in Africa, Asia and the Middle East

BARBARA BUTLER

kevin
mayhew

First published in 2003 by
KEVIN MAYHEW LTD
Buxhall, Stowmarket, Suffolk, IP14 3BW
E-mail: info@kevinmayhewltd.com

KINGSGATE PUBLISHING INC
1000 Pannell Street, Suite G, Columbia, MO 65201
E-mail: sales@kingsgatepublishing.com

© 2003 Barbara Butler

The right of Barbara Butler to be identified as the author of this work has been asserted by her in accordance with the Copyright, Designs and Patents Act 1988.

All rights reserved. No part of this publication may be reproduced, stored in a retrieval system, or transmitted, in any form or by any means, electronic, mechanical, photocopying, recording or otherwise, without the prior written permission of the publisher.

9 8 7 6 5 4 3 2 1 0

ISBN 1 84417 048 9
Catalogue No 1500576

Cover design by Angela Selfe
Edited by Peter Dainty
Typesetting by Richard Weaver
Printed and bound in Great Britain

Contents

Thanks	5
Foreword	7
Introduction	9

AFRICA

Desolation in Central Africa	19
Truth, Forgiveness and Reconciliation in South Africa	37
Water for Life in Tanzania	55
Moving and Growing in Kenya	69

ASIA

Solidarity and Sharing in Sri Lanka	87
Women at Work in South India	105
Suffering and Service in Pakistan	123
Healing and Hope in Bangladesh	137
Community and Service in Japan	147

THE MIDDLE EAST

Cross Roads in the Middle East	163
Bread in Egypt	181

Author's Mini Biography

Barbara Butler is the Executive Secretary of Christians Aware, an international and educational charity. She organises conferences and courses on issues of mission and development. She arranges for groups to visit and work in the developing world.

Dedication

For friends in the developing world who have taught me so much.

Thanks

The front cover painting and all the paintings in this book are the works of Winitha Fernando. Winitha is a Sri Lankan artist. She has won World Council of Churches awards and studied fine arts, pottery and stained glass in the UK. She has exhibited all over Europe and in America, as well as in Sri Lanka. I am grateful to Winitha for the inspiration of her work and for its inclusion here.

I am grateful to all the communities around the world who have accepted the Christians Aware groups and myself as guests in their homes and as sharers in some of their work over recent years.

I would like to thank Mano Rumalshah, the General Secretary of the United Society for the Propagation of the Gospel, for his advice on the chapter on Pakistan, where he was Bishop of Peshawar for ten years until 1998.

I would also like to thank Anand and Jessie Azir for their insights into the work of the Church of South India and Jessie especially for her on-going work with the women there.

I am grateful to John and Rita Bennett for their insights into life and work in Bangladesh where they lived and worked through the Methodist Church.

The contribution Donald Arden has made towards an understanding of the suffering caused by HIV/AIDS in Africa has been great and has given me resources to write the chapter on Central Africa.

Yohan and Malini Devananda have been steadfast workers in Sri Lanka and have made a huge contribution, Malini through her development work and Yohan through his commitment to the World Solidarity Forum.

There are many friends in Kenya who work for justice and peace, including Alfred Chipman, Godfrey Ngungire, Pauline Muturi, Stephen Wainyana, Timothy Ranji and Samuel Mwangi. My thanks go to them and to many others.

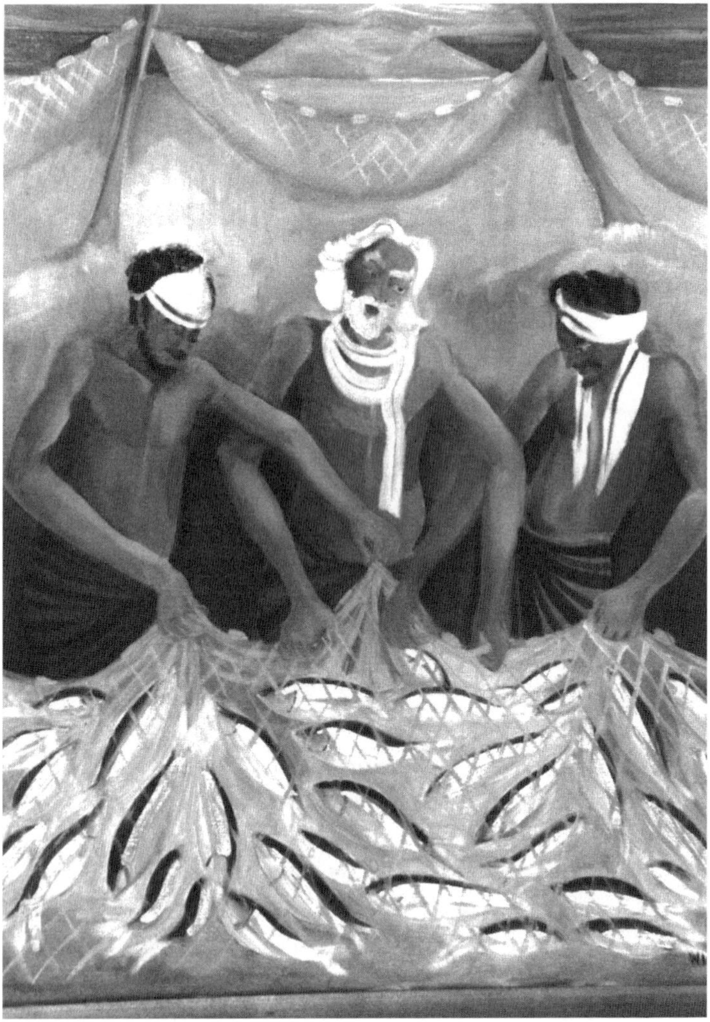

Foreword
by John Ramadhani

Windows into the World Church is a book written by Barbara Butler, Executive Secretary of an international and inter-denominational Christian organisation known as 'Christians Aware'. Barbara, through her many travels with her groups to different parts of the world, engaging themselves in helping local people in their self help projects, became keenly aware of the people they worked with, in the world church.

I first met Barbara and her group on one such expedition when they visited Tanzania more than a decade ago. They worked with our church group in a project or two before they moved on to another part of the country to undertake similar tasks. The work they did with our youth provided them with windows to look into our church and society and to learn something about us. That does not make them experts in respect of our situation but it does give them an awareness, essential if one is to love one's neighbour as oneself.

As a student at the Queen's Ecumenical College in Birmingham from 1973 to 1976, I found myself thrown into unfamiliar surroundings at first, with people from other parts of the world, with various shades of Christian belief, pledging to live together as one Christian family. We soon learnt that it was of paramount importance to try first to understand a neighbour's point of view in order to establish meaningful communication and working relationships. The future of our world as a global village lies in that direction.

This book is not meant to be specifically Anglican but inevitably there is more about the Anglican Church than about others. It includes chapters on South India, Kenya, Japan, Bangladesh, Tanzania, Sri Lanka, the Middle East, Zambia, South Africa and Malawi.

I sincerely commend this book to all those whose heartfelt desire is for a closer understanding of their multicultural neighbours in our global surroundings.

Bishop John Ramadhani has just retired as the Anglican Bishop of Zanzibar. Until 1998 he was the Archbishop of Tanzania.

Introduction

The front cover of this book includes a stained glass window of the traditional story of the three wise men taking gifts to the Christ child in the stable. It is the creation of a Sri Lankan artist, Winitha Fernando. What we can see when we look at the window is that the wise men are the ones giving gifts to the child and his family. They are the rich kings who have travelled from a long way away, perhaps from Persia. They are obviously rich and have gifts to give. The child Jesus and his family are obviously struggling. They are poor and so rejected that they had to ask to stay in a stable until the baby had been born, surrounded by animals. They are the poor who are receiving the gifts from the rich.

But if we look a little further into the window, and then through it, through to the truth it represents, we begin to realise that what is seen quickly and superficially is not the whole truth. There is giving and receiving, and some of it is from the kings to the child, but beyond that, and the kings themselves know this because they are kneeling to the child, the kings are receiving the greatest gift of all, the gift of new and everlasting life. The gift of the child is not something that could easily be included in the window, but it is there nevertheless. The gift of the child is not something that may easily be believed by observers who look at the window. It may only be known, understood and appreciated by those who go through the window to live the life that is offered, and thus to experience the endless truth that is touched on in the story and in the bright colour of the stained glass.

My hope is that this book will give those who read it an opportunity to look through some 'Windows into the World Church' and to experience a little of the real life of Christians in other parts of the world, with many and varied histories and cultures. My hope is that the glimpses of life I have offered, in only a few places, will lead some people to new understanding, appreciation and working together for the future of the one world we all share. The glimpses are into particular facets of life in the communities I have chosen. Different facets could have been explored but I have hopefully focused on those which are most representative.

Jesus' first sermon, in Nazareth, was of the gift of the good news he brought for the poor of the world.

> *The Spirit of the Lord is upon me. He has chosen me to preach the good news to the poor, to heal the sick and to release those who are in prison . . .*

All people are poor in one way or another, and in need of what God and other people may give. All are also equal in that they have something they can give to others.

Mother Teresa of Calcutta was someone who brought good news to the poor in the very recent past. She often spoke of only having the energy to do the work she did, work for the poorest of the poor, those who were the dying destitutes taken from the streets, because she saw the face of the Christ in them all. Through the ragged and dying people of Calcutta, who were, and are, mostly Hindus and Muslims, Mother Teresa was given new life and energy to do her work. She saw her relationship with the dying and the poor as an equal one between the children of God in that place. Once a visitor said to her, 'I couldn't do what you do for a million pounds'. 'Neither could I,' was her reply. 'I do it for the love of Christ.'

The gospel challenge to Christians is to relate to the total reality of any community, at home and anywhere in the world, not in a condemning way and not in a romantic way, but in a realistic way, learning to go through stained glass barriers and to recognise the good and the bad, the beautiful and the ugly, and to work within it all, with those who are already there, with the Christ who is already there.

The challenge is not to struggle to impose a particular way of life, or even Christianity, onto other people. The Christ who is the beginning and the end of all things does not need us to try to fit him into the world as it is, or even to speak up for him all the time.

What I believe Christians are called to do is to see the real world and people and to recognise the Christ who is there, in every place and person, and therefore to work to change the world, as partners with our fellow human beings, so that it is a fit place for the Christ, for every person.

Jesus' ministry, of bringing the good news to the poor, to all of us, was real and also realistic. Jesus' ministry could not have happened if he had not loved and been part of the world as he found it in the first place. It could not have happened if he had not seen himself as enabling others, in his lifetime and beyond.

For example, when Jesus spoke to the woman at the well he was speaking to a woman who was seen as unclean by the Jewish people, a Samaritan woman. Jesus should not, according to the tradition, have spoken to her, let alone have asked her for a drink of the polluted water. But he did speak, he went through the barriers of culture and tradition and focused his full attention upon her, seeing her as a real, true person, even though she had a questionable lifestyle, and moreover, he asked her to help him. He gave the gift of giving.

Jyoti Sahi is an artist who works from an ashram near Bangalore in South India. Jyoti has painted the woman at the well many times. One of the paintings I have seen shows Jesus as an Eastern holy man, towering over the poor woman at the well. But, the woman is painted in blue, and is part of the water springing out of the well. She is the one giving Jesus new life, new hope. She is the one who is serving him, and, in Indian culture, she is the one bringing the things of God to him, because in Indian culture blue is the colour of the gods.

Jesus' gift to the woman at the well was not a charity hand-out, but the gift of giving. The good news to the 'poor,' to all of us, is not that others will help, but that God is with, and in, every person, all have human dignity and all can, with friendship and encouragement, be givers as well as receivers.

Rabindranath Tagore, the great Bengali poet, wrote about a poor beggar woman standing by the side of the road with a begging bowl asking for gifts, when along the road came an Indian prince. He stopped in front of her and her hopes rose as she held out her bowl. But, after a pause, he asked her what she had to give to him. She was shocked, and after some time of her trying to persuade him to give to her and of him challenging her to give to him, she grudgingly gave him a few grains of rice, part of her evening meal. He continued his journey and she went off to cook the supper, when she noticed something shining in the bowl of rice. She picked out a few grains of pure gold, exactly the same number of grains as she had given to the prince. She was heartbroken, wishing that she had given all the rice.

Many Christians in India are from the Dalit groups. One of the gifts of the church to them has been the change it has made in their names which meant 'slave' or 'servant'. The names have been changed, so that instead of being called servant or slave, people are called, 'Servant of God', or 'Slave of Christ'. People thus have dignity and hope, and courage to be givers. I read about a woman who had worked as a stone cutter, who actually managed to become an MP for Bihar. When I go to Calcutta I meet Christian, Hindu and Muslim people who are teachers in night schools for the child workers. Some of the teachers came from bustee or slum families and achieved university education. The community I work with, the Young Men's Welfare Society, has existed for long enough now to have made this possible. Their work is very much to give people the tools to give to others, through the development of small businesses, nutrition and health programmes, the provision of clean water and above all, the education of the children. It is good to know that the Churches of North and South India are introducing programmes for reconciliation between people of the faiths of India. At no time in history has this been more necessary. One of my glimpses in this book is into the window of the Church of South India, to experience a little of the great contribution of the women to their people and country.

And what is true for India is true also for other parts of the world. In the churches in Africa it is the young, and especially the young women, who run the churches. They do not separate church life from the rest of life, but have a much more holistic approach, so that ordinary life comes into the churches, and God is in the cooking, farming and work for the communities. Work for the communities is not easy in many societies where the AIDS pandemic and all that follows from it dominates, and young people, and especially those between the ages of 15 and 24 years, are the sufferers as well as the servers. In Botswana for instance, a 15-year-old boy stands a greater than 80 per cent chance of dying from AIDS. I have included a glimpse of what it means to be a Christian and to live in an AIDS dominated society in parts of Central Africa. And yet the African churches are strong, growing, and full of young people. 'Isn't he heavy?' said a visitor to a young African boy carrying a large baby on his back. 'No, he's my brother,' came the reply. It's truth and love of that quality that we encounter when we go through the barriers of stained glass and into the new places.

The danger is that we fail to go through the windows, tending instead to continue to see the world from inside our own places and cultures, not really seeing other places, people and cultures except through glass and therefore not at all clearly, and often seeing no reason to listen or learn because in our heart of hearts we believe that our understanding of the world, and our way of doing things is the best way. It can be hard for many of us to realise that our ways and wisdoms are not the only ways and wisdoms.

At no time has listening been more important than in our world as it is now, since 11 September 2001. We can no longer inhabit our own places and expect others to understand us and fit in with us. It is vital that we make an effort to cease to be satisfied with stained glass, and to make ourselves go through the windows into the real world to meet the people. Mutual understanding and learning are essential for all our futures.

Listening is the greatest gift to others, the gift most likely to give new life, hope and the ability to do and to give in return. People who are not listened to, and are therefore not understood, become demoralised and even have doubts about their own worth as people. I have run conferences for refugees who have come to the UK from dire situations all over the world in recent years, and have learnt from them that what they long for is people to listen to their stories, stories which remind them that they are real and that they once had roots, a home and a future. The man from the Democratic Republic of the Congo who has lived in London for ten years now is typical when he says, 'I am only just beginning to feel like a real person again, now that I have work to do here, and friends who trust me'. The greatest gift we can give to the refugees in our communities is to listen to their stories, through which we will also become enriched.

Listening to other people's stories is important because it enables both listener and story teller to recognise and accept the truth, no matter how horrible it is. This became very clear when the Truth and Reconciliation Commission was sitting in South Africa. I have offered an insight into some of the work of the commission in my chapter on South Africa.

Without respectful and honest understanding and listening the many conflicts and divisions of the world today will never be healed. The divisions of the Middle East for instance will never be resolved so long as the people there, and also in the wider world, put the various groups into good and bad categories. It is vital to recognise that all the people of faith, Muslims, Jews and Christians, have suffered throughout history and continue to do so. It is not helpful to take sides and to see either the Jewish or the Palestinian cause as just. I have tried to bring this truth out in my chapter on the Middle East.

Through listening, understanding and working together we may all forge strong links with those who are very different. University students may develop friendships with those who have no formal education. Urban people may experience rural living and surviving. All encounters between people who are different from each other are opportunities to listen and learn, sometimes across huge divides of culture and religion. Together we may work humbly for love and justice in the world.

It is in this way that all of us may see and live in the real world the Christ is already part of, and seek to change it in partnership with others, so that it is a fit place for him and for all people.

AFRICA

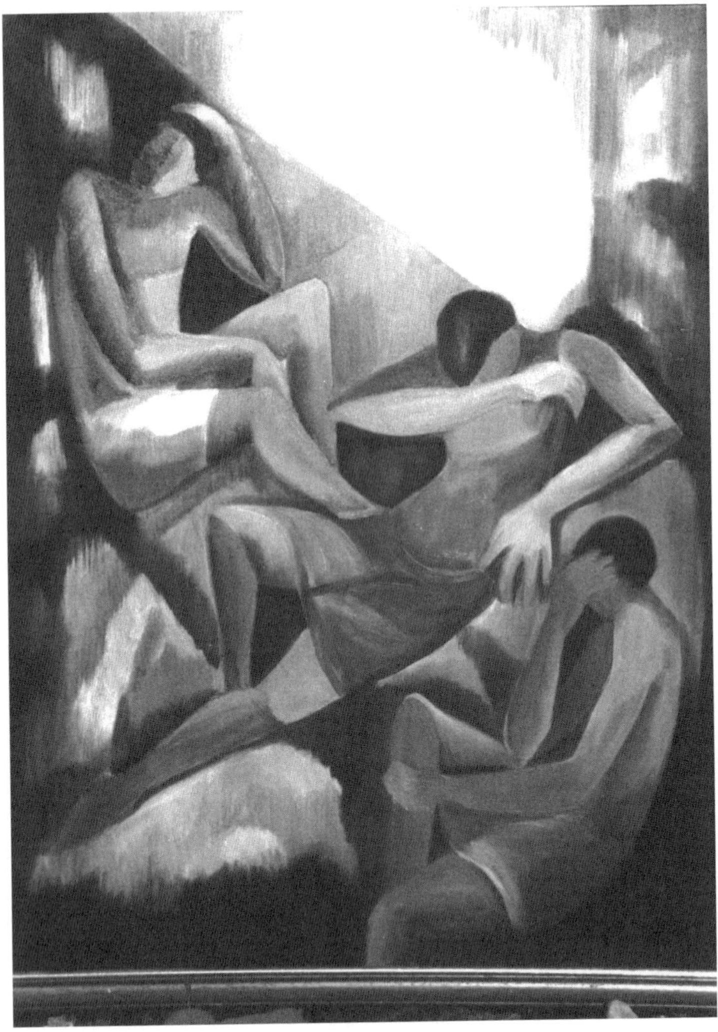

Desolation in Central Africa

And he took with him Peter and the two sons of Zebedee, and began to be sorrowful and very heavy.
St Matthew 26:37

AIDS today in Africa is claiming more lives than the sum total of all wars, famines and floods and ravages of such deadly diseases as malaria. It is devastating families and communities, overwhelming and depleting health care services and robbing schools of both students and teachers.
Nelson Mandela[1]

The HIV pandemic is one of the greatest health, security and human development crises facing the planet. It kills millions of adults in their prime. It fractures and impoverishes families, weakens workforces, turns millions of children into orphans, and threatens the social and economic fabric of communities and the political stability of nations. In just two decades AIDS has become a global emergency of catastrophic proportions.[2]

A friend who lived and worked in Zambia for many years returned and agreed to give a talk on his experiences and on the country and people. When someone asked him what the impact of AIDS related illnesses was on the people he surprised everyone by replying, 'There is not much impact, they are just another way of dying'.

One of the devastating experiences for visitors to sub-Saharan Africa today is indeed that dying is the norm and that, though it is not obvious, AIDS related illnesses are

---

1. Nelson Mandela in the USPG pack *Chance of a Lifetime*, published by USPG.
2. Catholic Bishops' Conference for England and Wales.

increasingly responsible. It is not unusual to find the young children being looked after by people in their 70s and even older, because the middle generation has died out. Some visitors are even taken out into small gardens by children to see the graves of the parents. Usually it is an old woman who is looking after many small children, and managing to keep herself and them alive by doing any odd piece of work she can think of, including brewing and selling beer, or cutting firewood and selling it. One old woman in Malawi said recently, 'I have been bringing up children for 50 years and I am so tired now. My husband is old and cannot do anything'.[1]

Sometimes the old people have also died and children are cared for by children.

HIV stands for human immunodeficiency virus. It is passed on from person to person, mainly through sexual intercourse. The virus depletes a person's immune system so that they can no longer protect themselves against a whole variety of illnesses. AIDS stands for acquired immune deficiency syndrome which covers these illnesses.

Today, in the early twenty-first century between 34 and 40 million people in the world are HIV positive and there are 18,000 new infections every day. Sub-Saharan Africa has 70 per cent of the global total of HIV positive people.[2]

AIDS related illnesses are the main cause of death in sub-Saharan Africa and its casualities are in every age group except the very old. One of the main ways in which HIV is contracted is through unprotected sex, which means that the main group affected is the most sexually active group, the young heterosexual adults, those society would normally rely on to bring up the children and to do some of the most important work. HIV can also be contracted through infected blood transfusions and through intravenous drug injections.

---

1. Donald Arden, *Christians Aware* magazine, Winter 2001.
2. United Nations Programme on HIV/AIDS, December 2000.

AIDS has left more than 12 million African orphans.[1] Zambia has the highest proportion of AIDS orphans in the world. Here 23 per cent of all children under 15 have lost one or both parents to AIDS related illness. Traditionally African orphans would be taken into the extended family, but this is now becoming impossible, as the number of orphans is growing and the number of carers is shrinking. The problem of street children, those for whom the street has become their real home, is growing rapidly in Africa. Emmanuel Kalunga is nine years old, his mother has died and he lives with his grandmother who is disabled. His grandmother said of Emmanuel, 'He is quiet and stays alone a lot – he cries sometimes'. Many of Emmanuel's friends live on the streets during the daytime because there is no one to arrange for them to go to school. His grandmother worries that she will die and Emmanuel then will not go to school.[2]

Between 1 and 1.4 million children under the age of 15 are infected by HIV worldwide, mostly during pregnancy, through the birth process or through breast feeding. The dangers of breast feeding are a nightmare for mothers and health workers, because any alternative is also dangerous in environments where bottles are not easy to clean and where the powdered baby milk is expensive. Eighty per cent of the infected children are living in Africa.[3] Children develop AIDS related illness much more quickly than adults and half the infected children die before they reach the age of two years, while 80 per cent will die before they reach five years.

There are many factors in the spread of HIV and perhaps one of the main ones is simply poverty. In poor situations people are ground down, always tired and not necessarily aware of the implications of their lifestyles on their health.

---

1. United Nations Programme on HIV/AIDS, December 2000.
2. *No excuses. Facing up to sub-Saharan Africa's AIDS orphans crisis*, Christian Aid.
3. *The State of the World's Children, 2002,* UNICEF, 2002.

They are also more rapidly weakened by disease than those who are well fed.

The Rt Revd Peter Nyanja, Anglican Bishop of Lake Malawi, an area which is suffering severe famine because of poor harvests, erratic weather and poor planning said recently:

> *I am 61 and I have never before seen a time of disaster and crisis facing Malawi, in the areas of hunger, poverty and disease. While we are fighting the HIV/AIDS scourge and poverty, we have been saddened and overtaken by hunger and starvation . . . Sunday services are reducing in number as people are staying home because they cannot survive a church service with an empty stomach. The giving has completely reduced. This means that clergy in the Diocese will soon receive no pay – in fact from April 2002 I do not know where salaries will come from.*[1]

In a pastoral letter, Malawi's seven Roman Catholic bishops attacked the current government on a number of issues including its handling of the hunger crisis. The letter was applauded by thousands of worshippers when it was read out in churches everywhere on Easter Day 2002.

Harriet's life in Karonga Square Township, an official housing area on the edge of Lusaka, the capital city of Zambia, is a life of poverty and deprivation. The only bright spot for her is the widow's group she is a member of, where the women meet and support each other, helping with shopping and caring for the children.

> *The red-earth streets are full of children, dogs and the occasional chicken. They are also fringed with rubbish, (there is no collection), not much grows, and when you collect water*

---

1. Peter Nyanja was quoted by Revd Mary Vickers in the *World Church Focus*.

from the communal pump, you have to pay 100 kwacha for the privilege. Harriet lives in a dark room round the back of a broken down house, with four children of her own and one grandchild. She herself is HIV positive, with many health problems. Her husband died of AIDS, and also her eldest daughter. Now Joel, her 19 year old son, is sick. When we arrive Joel is huddled under the cover on the only bed, tired and hungry after going looking for work. But, there is no food in the house. Harriet used to sell eggs, but then she had to spend the egg money on the rent, and she has never been able to get going again. Honestly she can't see that she ever will, with the triple burden of rent, sickness and the family. Also, she is so tired . . .[1]

The churches are now introducing some teaching programmes to help people combat AIDS related illness, but it is late in the day and much of the damage has already been done. Earlier hesitation was partly due to shyness and partly perhaps to a misguided Puritanism which meant that sex was never talked about in church groups. I can remember about five years ago asking whether the churches were doing anything in relation to HIV/AIDS in more than one African country, only to be told that there was no problem. Sometimes Christians have been, and some still are, judgemental about those who have HIV, saying, 'People who get HIV/AIDS have no one but themselves to blame'.[2]

It is not surprising that many people with HIV have kept their condition a secret, making it impossible to help them.

Lack of work opportunities at home often propels men into the urban areas where they are alone and therefore vulnerable to dangerous sexual encounters. Rates of HIV/AIDS infection are generally worse along trade routes and in border

---

1. *AIDS and the African Churches: exploring the challenges*, Gillian Paterson, Christian Aid, 2001.
2. Quoted by Revd Dr. Susan Cole-King after a visit to Malawi in 2000.

towns, where there are often many sex workers. Any kind of unrest, including war, when people are unstable and uncertain about the future, will create a climate where normal morals break down and unsafe sex is practised more widely. Sometimes in poor environments the dire unemployment leads people to despair, so that even when they know the cost of casual sexual relationships they do not care, because they may feel they have no future.

Sometimes women become desperate to find work so that they can feed their families and they turn to sex as a way of earning some money. This is very obviously extremely dangerous but the answer to it is not to ask the women to stop doing it, but rather for church people and others to work to create alternative employment. Sometimes young girls are persuaded into sexual relationships by men who, because they are promiscuous, are likely to pass HIV on to them. Sometimes the young girls are coerced into sex, but sometimes they are caring for younger brothers and sisters alone, because their parents have died of AIDS related illness, and they, like slightly older women, are desperate to earn money. They may be desperate for food for their families and also for fees for education. Sometimes the exchange does not involve money at all, when sex is given in return for food.

The HIV/AIDS pandemic has affected every aspect of life in sub-Saharan Africa. The economy of the whole region has suffered for many reasons. One important reason is that the young adults, those who would normally do most of the work, are those who are most affected by the pandemic. In the urban areas the skilled and professional groups are affected badly. In the rural areas the land is being neglected, fields are left uncultivated and stray cattle are roaming around. In some areas of Central Africa the forests are again taking over the landscape. And so a vicious circle of poverty, illness and more poverty is allowed to develop.

Education has suffered as the teachers are dying and children cannot go to school because either they are caring for sick parents, brothers and sisters, are sick themselves or have no money. A 2002 study among commercial farm workers in Zimbabwe showed that 50 per cent of children whose parents had died of AIDS related illnesses were forced to leave school. There were no AIDS orphans at all in the secondary schools.[1] The situation in Zimbabwe is worsening by the day, as more and more farm workers are turned away from the white owned farms, and have no way of earning a living. The numbers of people involved are in the region of 780,000, and many of them are very young or very old and also homeless.[2] This is a sad development in a country where there were so many hopes of good things when independence came in 1980.

The health systems of Africa have been in decline since the 1980s, due to the burden of the countries seeking, mostly unsuccessfully, to pay off the debts owed to the rich creditor nations. The reforms demanded by the International Monetary Fund and the World Bank, including the structural adjustment programmes, imposed on most of Africa, left countries with little to put into health, education or transport. Often the rural health services have been utterly destroyed and the health personnel have disappeared or died from AIDS related illnesses. If a health clinic is accessible to people sometimes they have to wait too long for attention because they are poor and cannot raise the money needed. In Zambia for instance the health treatment is not free, because the government only spends less than $10 per person, per year, on health. The World Health Organisation has suggested that $60 per person, per year, would be reasonable.[3]

---

1. Christian Aid.
2. Estimate of the Zimbabwe Community Development Trust.
3. *The Bitterest Pill of All. The collapse of Africa's Health Systems*, Save the Children.

Susan Cole-King[1] said that what was most needed in response to the suffering of Africa caused by the HIV/AIDS pandemic was for the churches to work to change attitudes. There is the need to understand that HIV/AIDS is a 'gospel issue' and therefore a priority for the whole church.

The churches of Central Africa were slow to do anything about HIV/AIDS, but they have recently woken up to the tragedy in their midst and are struggling to find ways to respond, to seek to change attitudes and also to challenge government.

Central Africa includes Zambia, Zimbabwe, Malawi and Botswana. The Anglican Province was founded in 1955 to cover the four countries. All four countries are predominantly Christian, with some traditional religions, some of which are closer to Christianity than others. The only other major world religion with a significant following is Islam, which has always been a large minority religion in Malawi but which is now growing in the other countries also, especially in Zambia. Today there is a Muslim President in Malawi, following the multi-party elections at the end of the 30-year dictatorship of Dr Hastings Banda, who dominated his country following its independence in 1964.

The Roman Catholic Church is the largest church in the region. The largest Protestant Church is a union of the churches planted by the South African Dutch Reformed Church, the Church of Scotland and the Free Church of Scotland. The Anglican Church is small in numbers but makes an important contribution. It has been a source of unity over the years when political divisions were great. For example, because Zimbabwe did not achieve its independence until 1980, the Anglican province, including as it did countries which became independent in the early 1960s, was able to be a sign of hope and also a challenge.

---

1. Susan Cole-King, who died in the Summer of 2001, was the Chief Medical Officer of UNICEF and an Anglican priest.

The Anglican presence in Central Africa grew from the appeal David Livingstone made to the students of the universities of Oxford and Cambridge to go to serve in an exciting and vital mission to the people of the area he knew and loved. The Anglo-Catholic Universities Mission to Central Africa was formed in 1857 and its missionaries have played a key role in the development of the region. In 1965 it was united with the Society for the Propagation of the Gospel to form the USPG.[1] The model of mission put into practice by the UMCA was that its missionaries went to Africa to be part of Africa, and part of the church there. They were known for living with the local people, learning the languages, translating the Bible and prayer books into the local languages and generally taking root in the local soil. They had an important role to play in the abolition of slavery in East and Central Africa, in the raising of standards of health and in the introduction of education. They worked with the people to create a local and indigenous ministry which was developed when the countries achieved their independence.

The mostly peaceful movement towards independence for the countries of Central Africa has been seen by some historians as, partly at least, the result of the contribution of the UMCA, because it worked with people as equals. The teaching in the mission stations was that people were free people, who were there to grow towards independence. There were some skirmishes in the years before political independence was achieved, but on the whole the movement was supported by the churches, including most UMCA missionaries. Perhaps the two most famous ordained people to support the movement to independence were in Zambia. They were Oliver Green-Wilkinson, who was Archbishop of Central Africa from 1962 until his death in 1970, and the Methodist Minister on the Copperbelt, Colin Morris. They were both in close

---

1. *Three Centuries of Mission. The United Society for the Propagation of the Gospel, 1701-2000*, Daniel O'Connor, Continuum, 2000.

contact with Kenneth Kaunda, a keen Christian who became the first President of the independent country in 1964.[1] The link between the churches and the state in Zambia was always strong. Special state services were always held in Lusaka Cathedral. When Kenneth Kaunda and the United National Independence Party or UNIP, were challenged by the Movement for Multi-party Democracy a debate was held in the cathedral in July 1991, and when the elections were held later in the same year the churches played a large role in the monitoring process. In October 1991 the MMD won the elections and President Chiluba took over. An ecumenical service was held in Lusaka Cathedral to mark the occasion.

Following independence in three of the Central African countries, in 1964 in Malawi and Zambia and in 1966 in Botswana, efforts were made to train African clergy and by 1973 they were the majority of ordinands in training, though in recent years there have been fewer vocations. The churches of Central Africa have kept their tradition of training in many disciplines and vocations alive and this, together with their early commitment to education and health, and the tradition which was developed by church workers of all backgrounds, of working with the people rather than for the people, meant that after a very slow start the churches throughout the region were able to take responsibility and to make a useful contribution to those suffering from the HIV/AIDS pandemic.

Many Christians in Africa struggle to make sense of the suffering they live with in relation to a God they have always understood as a loving God. Many people are asking, 'Where is God in the HIV/AIDS pandemic?' Some people are beginning to find the answer in the Christ who came to earth and shared in the life of the people, including the suffering of the people, and continues to share life and suffering, from the

---

1. *A Humanist in Africa*, Kenneth Kaunda, Longmans, 1966.
   Zambia Shall be Free, Kenneth Kaunda, Heinemann, 1962.

beginning to the end of all things. The Christ who is the one Christians see in the hungry, the sick and the prisoners, is also to be met in the people who have HIV and AIDS related illnesses.

Christian hope is there in Central Africa, and it is there in brave and hard-working people who give their lives for their friends.

Donald Arden, who was Archbishop of Central Africa from 1973 to 1981, suggested that perhaps the most pressing challenge there is to develop Christian compassion within the worshipping community. The churches could work towards being safe places, where people could admit to being HIV positive or to having AIDS related illness, knowing that they would be loved, accepted and cared for. This challenge of course applies to Christian communities worldwide. Many Christians still seem to find it easier to take an attitude of judgement than one of love. The example from the Gospel story about the prodigal son, whose loving father rushed out to greet him unconditionally on his return home, is an encouraging one. There are also many people with HIV in Africa who are the completely innocent, having contracted the virus through infected blood transfusions or through the birth process and do not need forgiveness but only love.

If the churches can bring together the love and care for people with HIV with counselling of them they will perhaps encourage openness and begin to educate the wider community, thus encouraging people to go for tests, to take greater personal responsibility for their actions and to show more love and compassion for their partners.

Susan Cole-King travelled to Malawi in 2000 and found that there was openness to learning and to action, because there had been an official programme of study in the Anglican Church. Many of the congregations have set up HIV/AIDS committees and the volunteers have raised money to help orphans. They also visit the sick and offer counselling. Attitudes are in fact changing as people move from condemnation towards an understanding that people living with HIV need love and acceptance.

The example set by the churches in their recent work with AIDS orphans is being taken up by others. For example 'Children in Distress' is an organisation in Zambia which is not tied to a church but which relies on volunteers from any walk of life. The organisation keeps a register of orphans and of any guardians, so that when guardians die their children may be taken into the homes of others. Some people are looking after eight or more children. The organisation offers some schooling for children who could not afford the very small fees to attend government schools. It also offers gardening and brick making.

It is encouraging that the Malawi Council of Churches has given a strong lead by running ecumenical workshops for the priests and ministers. They have also produced a statement confessing their past failures. They have committed themselves to:

> ... *promote behaviour change; provide care to orphans, the sick, widows and widowers; to be open and talk and teach about AIDS; to promote the creation of hope and to ensure economic empowerment.*

The Southern Malawi Synod passed an important statement committing the diocese to several steps:
- Breaking the silence, removing the stigma and being open about AIDS.
- Seeing sexuality as a gift from God.
- Promoting pre-marriage testing.
- Empowering girls to refuse unwanted sex.
- Influencing cultural practices that contribute to the spread of AIDS.
- Recognising that there is a role for condoms.
- Affirming that God loves, and especially, sinners.

- Teaching that nothing, even death, can separate us from the love of God.

Until recently the churches have all been opposed to the use of condoms in the fight against the spread of HIV and many still are opposed to this way forward. The Roman Catholic Church is especially vehement in its opposition to condoms, as it is everywhere in the world, as part of its teaching on the ideal of faithful relationships within marriage. Some governments, including the Government of Malawi, have encouraged the use of condoms, and many of the churches have been very critical. The fear is that condoms will give some people an excuse for promiscuous behaviour and may even lead to more people who are HIV positive. Some Christians and some churches are beginning to see that there is a role for condoms, and particularly within marriage, to protect one partner. Some Christians are beginning to say that the use of condoms can reduce the spread of HIV/AIDS. However there is also the realisation that condoms may be unreliable.[1] One of the other problems is that they are expensive and don't last, they are difficult to distribute in the African context and especially in rural areas. Furthermore, many people don't like them.

An ecumenical team from Sheffield spent three months in Malawi in 2000 when they visited St Luke's Church, Mpinganjila near Mangochi on the southern lakeshore and saw an inspiring HIV/AIDS project run by the Mothers' Union. The parish priest, Maurice Malasa is very supportive. He works for the Bible Society in translating the Scriptures into the Yao language. He is also translating the HIV/AIDS pamphlets issued by the Ministry of Health into Yao, as well as extracts from *One New Humanity*, by Anne Bayley, a priest and surgeon who worked for many years in Zambia

---

1. *The Truth about AIDS*, Dr Patrick Dixon, Kingsway Publications, 1994.

and who was one of the earliest people to recognise the HIV virus.[1]

The parish has nine churches and 2000 orphans, most of whom live with their very poor and elderly grandparents. Every Saturday a large number of the orphans meet with the Mothers' Union members in the church. They are taught about health and hygiene and how to prevent the spread of the HIV virus. The Mothers' Union members grow vegetables to provide a meal for the children and also to raise money for their support.

One of the challenges to the members of the Mothers' Union is to work with the Yao tribal elders and to encourage them to change the methods used at initiation ceremonies and to make sure that the instruments used for male circumcision are surgically clean. The custom of young women and men experimenting with sex, which is part of the traditional culture, is also being discouraged because it spreads HIV. The Mothers' Union has had a lot of opposition to its challenge to the traditions of the people. Most of the Yao are Muslims, and many of them also feel that the teaching of the children is not simply to combat HIV/AIDS but also to proselytise. An effort is now being made by the Mothers' Union to raise money to build a new hall, so that the children do not have to meet in the church. The women are making the bricks and also firing them. They are struggling to help the Yao people to see that their only wish is for the children to be healthy. The Mothers' Union has also recently hired a surgeon to perform the circumcisions. They are trying to raise enough money for electricity and a water pump, so that their crops will be bigger and their contribution to the health of the people will be greater.

The future of Africa depends upon its young people surviving the HIV/AIDS pandemic and many young people all over sub-Saharan Africa are beginning to take responsibility

---

1. *One New Humanity*, Anne Bayley, SPCK, 1996.

for their survival and futures, for the sake of everyone. 'Treasuring the Gift' is the title of a youth discussion course, written by a group of young Zambians. It is perhaps unique in that it has been written by young people for young people. It is ecumenical and also inter-faith. It was published by the Lusaka Interfaith Networking Group which links in the Islamic community with the Christian Council, the Catholic Episcopal Conference and the Evangelical Fellowship. The aim of the group is to '... put aside doctrinal and denominational differences in order to work together in the fight against HIV/ AIDS'.

The notes at the end of the 140-page discussion course are interesting:

> *We should try to commit as few sins as possible ... If we commit adultery or fornication using a condom, we commit one sin only. But if we do the same without a condom, we commit two sins: sexual immorality, plus the danger of causing the death of our sexual partner or of ourselves.*
>
> *God has a perfect way that he wants us to follow. However, the religious tradition has many examples of God acknowledging that humans often fail to follow his perfect way, and providing another way eg. tolerance of divorce; tolerance of the Israelites wanting to be ruled by kings.*
>
> *Even when we do wrong, eg. fornication, God wants to shield us from the full consequences of our wrong actions, and condoms are one way of doing this.*

One way the churches have pioneered of working with young people in HIV/AIDS education is drama. This is done for the sake of the actors themselves, when they are asked to take on a role which is different from their own, and to realise what the other person is going through. It is also done for the sake of the audiences, who may learn more easily from dramatic performances than from other presentations.[1]

St Francis Hospital in Katete in Eastern Zambia is run jointly by the Anglican and Roman Catholic Churches and has patients from all over the country and region. It is well known for training nurses. One of its recent developments is the AIDS education programme which relies heavily on drama. The AIDS patients normally live at home and receive basic treatment. There is good support from Katete for the AIDS orphans.

The recent work of the churches of all denominations in Central Africa for the fight against the HIV/AIDS pandemic and against the suffering caused to the people is very impressive. There is much that can still be done to relieve the desolation which hangs over the entire region like a blanket of despair, and some of it can be done in partnership with the churches around the world.

It is vital that the poverty of much of Africa is alleviated and that people in Africa and people in the developed world unite to achieve this; including relief from debt, the reform of the international trade rules, the enabling of the poor countries to receive the medicines they need, an increase in international aid and a further raising of awareness of the need for education for health.

The need for healthy women who live and work as the equals of men, in their sexual lives, in their homes and nations, is desperate.[2] No opportunity should be missed by the African people, but also by visitors to Africa to affirm this and to work for it. Some of the churches could do more to work for the dignity and equality of women as part of their work for a future which is 'good news' for all the African people.

---

1. *Confronting AIDS together*, Anne Skelmerud and Christopher Tusibira, Centre for Partnershsip in Development, Oslo.
2. *Love in a Time of AIDS*, Gillian Patterson, Risk Books, 1996.

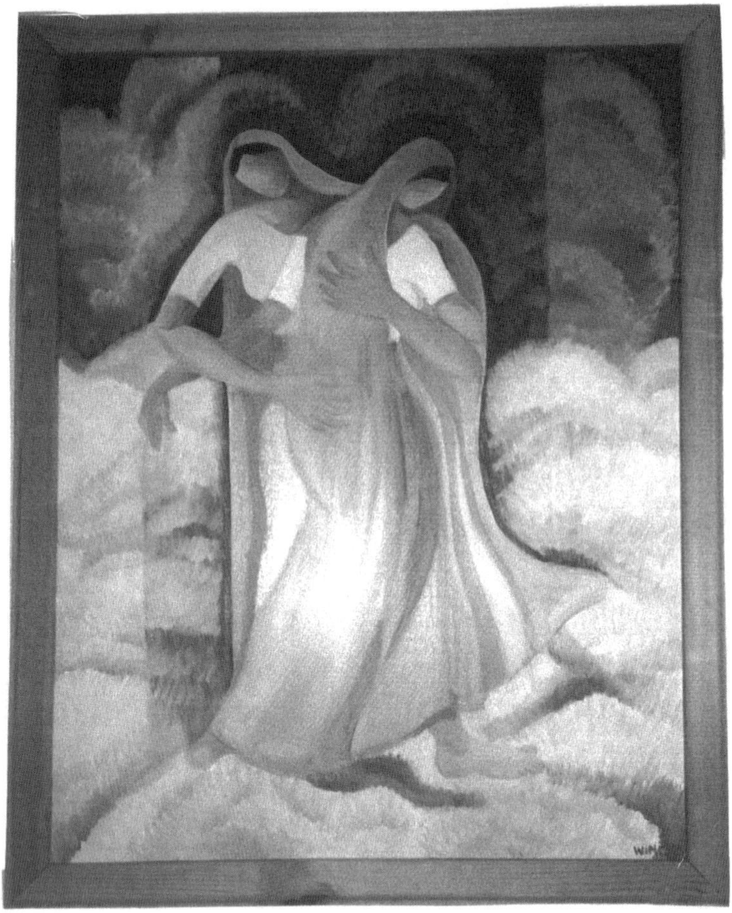

Truth, Forgiveness and Reconciliation in South Africa

What does the Lord require of you? To act justly and to love mercy and to walk humbly with your God.

Micah 6:8

While we will not forget the brutality of apartheid, we will not want Robben Island to be a monument of our hardship and suffering. We would want it to be a triumph of the human spirit against the forces of evil. A triumph of wisdom and largeness of spirit against small minds and pettiness; a triumph of courage and determination over human frailty and weakness; a triumph of the new South Africa over the old.

Ahmed Kathrada

Robben Island in Table Bay off Cape Town, once a prison, a place of misery, horror and death, a stark symbol of the distressing truth that the human race, ordinary people, can and do oppress each other, causing unimaginable suffering, is now, following the 1994 democratic elections and the ending of apartheid in South Africa, a place of peace and beauty, and a symbol of the possibility of the forgiveness and reconciliation that are beginning to happen in some people in the new country. A place of stones is the opportunity for pilgrims to the island to add a stone and to remember someone who died in the struggle for freedom. The island is a symbol of all that is hoped for in the future.

A very early prisoner on Robben Island was Nxele. He was a Xhosa diviner who vehemently opposed the spread of Christianity because he felt, as many others have felt and still feel, that it was alien to African spirituality. He wanted people to enjoy their natural instincts and to dance, make love and live to the full. He saw Christianity as a miserable alternative of sober living and praying. In 1819 he led an attack of Xhosa warriors on Grahamstown, believing that the bullets fired against him would turn to water. He was sent to Robben Island and drowned when he tried to swim to freedom.

Nelson Mandela is the most famous person to have been a prisoner on Robben Island. He was more fortunate than Nxele. He was a prisoner for 27 years, for opposing the apartheid regime of the Nationalist Government, but he lived to forgive his enemies and to write about his experiences. He described Robben Island in his time there as, 'The harshest, most iron-fisted outpost in the South African penal system'.[1]

When he became the President of his country Nelson Mandela invited his white gaoler from Robben Island to attend the inauguration. He and others were shining examples of the triumph of the human spirit in a time of darkness, and of the possibility of people forgiving those who have persecuted them. Desmond Tutu, who has retired as the Anglican Archbishop of Cape Town, has written of Nelson Mandela,

> *This man, who had been vilified and hunted down as a dangerous fugitive and incarcerated for three decades, was transformed into the embodiment of forgiveness and reconciliation, and had most of those who had hated him eating out of his hand.*[2]

The Churches of South Africa were not all on the side of all the people in the development of their country. The position of the Churches in relation to separate development or apartheid, its removal and the struggle for the truth and for forgiveness and reconciliation has been as varied as it is possible to be. There was no Christian view of apartheid in

---

1. *Long Walk to Freedom*, Nelson Mandela, Little, Brown and Company, 1994.
2. *No Future Without Forgiveness*, Desmond Tutu, Rider, 1999, p. 7.

South Africa before 1994 because Christians were in every camp. The white community for instance could have been broken down into those who sacrificed themselves for freedom, along with their black brothers and sisters, those who supported apartheid, believing it to be the will of God, and those who hovered between the two extreme positions. The same was true of the Coloured and of the Black communities.

The presence of the white community has been a dominating one in South Africa unlike most of the rest of Africa. Immigration from Europe began before the seventeenth century and by the beginning of the nineteenth century the Boers, from Dutch, German and Huguenot backgrounds, thought of themselves as African, and not as expatriate people who were living temporarily in another country. They did not, as a few others in other parts of Africa did, learn the local African languages and become part of the indigenous culture, but rather they attached their own folk culture to Africa. Part of this was their Dutch Reformed Church, influenced by Calvinism. Dutch Reformed thinking was based on separation and hierachy. At an early stage they opposed the work of George Schmidt, an eighteenth-century Moravian who proclaimed a Gospel of the grace and love of God for all people. They severed their links with Holland and started their own conservative college at Stellenbosch. They gradually developed separate churches for the separate racial groups, and thus laid the foundations for the Nationalist policy of separate development or apartheid.

English settlers in South Africa always remained a separate community from the Boers, and their Christianity was an extension of the Christianity of the British Isles. The Church in South Africa was influential in the convening of the first Lambeth Conference in 1867. Some English speaking missionaries always challenged the separation of peoples which was encouraged by the Dutch Reformed Church and championed the dignity of all the people, though sometimes in practice this was through separate development.

Some African rulers even invited English missionaries into their domains, as they saw them as protection against the Boers. A good example of this is Mosheshwe of the Basotho people. This course of action was quickly seen to be a mistake, as the missionaries seemed to be against many aspects of traditional culture, including some of the initiation ceremonies, polygamy and bride price. They also attracted not only Afrikaner incursions but also British imperialists, especially after the discovery of diamonds and gold. Some must have come to think that Nxele was right to oppose Christianity.

The Christian missions gave a home to many of the people who had escaped from the Zulu wars of Shaka and from the Xhosa wars with British and Afrkaans settlers. Some African people were naturally attracted to Christianity and others, like Nxele, were against it. It is perhaps impossible to decide why there were these differences of response; some might have been due to personality differences and others to cultural and historical differences. Whatever the reasons, the differences affected the development of the church and the history of the country.

Ntsikana was the councillor to the Xhosa chief who advised the acceptance of European rule and of Christianity. He even composed hymns and greatly influenced a large number of Xhosa to become Christian. The cattle killing movement of 1857 occurred because a young girl prophesied that if the cattle were killed and the maize was not planted the ancestors would be resurrected and there would be great prosperity. When the prophecy failed there was famine, loss of confidence and a great movement of people onto white farms and into the churches.

The Anglican, Methodist and Presbyterian Churches offered a good education, including the famous Scottish mission at Lovedale. Fort Hare College was established near to Lovedale in 1916 and gave excellent university education to African people from all over the continent until apartheid legislation made it into a tribal college in 1956. A tradition of excellence in education grew up amongst the Xhosa people, some of whom were the founding fathers of the great campaigns to end apartheid in the mid-twentieth century.

Christian education had a big share in the movement which led to the passionate witness and protest in the apartheid era and to the development of 'black theology'.[1] Black theology, closely linked to the black consciousness movement, grew naturally among educated black Christians who struggled for wholeness, as people loved by God and as potential citizens of a unified country where they would be the equals of their white neighbours. After an initial period of separation, when African culture and blackness were strongly focused on and affirmed, those who developed this thinking played an important part in the development of the real fellowship and commitment shared by many Christians across all the races in South Africa today. Many have worked very hard to demonstrate to all the people of South Africa that they are all loved by God, and are all equal in status and value.

A lot of the hard work is still being done to undo the psychological damage to many of the people in the apartheid era. Many people had come to believe that there was something wrong with them because they were black, and this made them fear and hate those who treated them badly. Even Desmond Tutu himself was heard, at the height of the apartheid regime, to ask in desperation, 'O God, do you hate us?'

There were surprisingly many ordinary South Africans who were as magnanimous as Nelson Mandela and the other great spirits who forgave their persecutors when democracy came in 1994. There is the well known story of the black man who cast his vote and then said, 'Today I became a human being'. The restoration of human dignity meant that many

---

1. *The Church Struggle in South Africa*, John W. de Gruchy, SPCK, 1979.

people were so restored that they desperately wanted to be loving and generous. Desmond Tutu has said that African culture creates people who are human because they belong to the community and that therefore they long to be ungrudgingly open-hearted and handed to those around them.

However, some people in South Africa felt, and perhaps a few still feel, that the atrocities committed were so great that the perpetrators should be, whenever possible, brought to trial and punished. Gillian Slovo, the daughter of Ruth First and Jo Slovo, has written about her parents' role in the struggle for freedom in South Africa and about her mother's assassination.[1] She now lives in England and was invited to South Africa to listen to the testimony of those who killed her mother. In an interview following her return to England she said that she was grateful that the truth had been expressed, but she could not forgive or feel reconciled to her mother's killers. There are many like her. Desmond Tutu, the person chosen to chair the Truth and Reconciliation Commission by Nelson Mandela and the Government of National Unity has said that for many people the pragmatic reasons for the attempts at truth and reconciliation had to be emphasised. He wrote,

> *There would have been no negotiated settlement and so no new and democratic South Africa had the negotiators on one side insisted that all perpetrators would be brought to trial. While the Allies could pack up and go home after Nuremberg, we in South Africa had to live with one another.*[2]

The very existence of the Truth and Reconciliation Commission and some of its successful work is quite remarkable when the

---

1. *Every Secret Thing*, Gillian Slovo, Little, Brown and Company, 1997.
2. *No Future Without Forgiveness*, Desmond Tutu, Rider, 1999, p. 25.

history of the apartheid years is considered. This history does not make easy reading, including as it does the up-rooting and separation of the communities for every aspect of their lives, the creation of the bantustans. and all the other legislation which immobilised and weakened those who were not white. White people were damaged by apartheid also of course, but the psychological damage to the non-whites was immeasurable.

District Six, at the foot of Table Mountain in Cape Town, was an example of a very lively, multi-racial and inter-faith community before the Nationalist Government came to power in 1948. And after that it was split up, and the Coloured, Indian and African people moved away to distant townships. In 1966, as part of the Group Areas Act, sections of the area were declared for white occupation only and most of the housing the other people had lived in was destroyed. Many people who had homes in District Six were naturally devasted when they had to leave and go to strange and inhospitable places. Many of them died very unhappily in exile. There were many more, living and dying in exile in the separate settlements and bantustans in the South Africa of the apartheid era.

Khayelitsha, meaning 'New Home' in Xhosa, was founded on the Cape Flats in 1986 following the destruction of the squatter camp of Crossroads. Its creation was controversial. At the time when it was built, it was used as a means of excluding certain selected people from the city centre, so that they had to travel to the town for work and for medical needs. It was very racist and it still provides many problems for those who live there.

There was also the violence of the apartheid era, as people protested against cruel laws, including the Sharpeville massacre of 21 March 1960, when 69 people were killed, mostly shot in the back, by police, when they were in a peaceful crowd of about 20,000 people who were demonstrating against the pass laws. In the Soweto uprising of 16 June 1976 10,000 or more unarmed schoolchildren went to Orlando West High School early in the morning to demonstrate against Afrikaans as the language of education. The police threw a tear gas cannister and some of the children reacted by throwing stones. The police then shot into the crowd of children and 13-year-old Hector Peterson and another child were killed. Protests spread throughout South Africa and by the end of June 176 people were dead, 1000 injured and 908 arrested. The violence quickly spread to other regions.

There were all the people who were killed in detention over the years, including the famous Steve Biko, who founded the Black Consciousness movement, but also many others, whose names will never be remembered. There were also the atrocities committed by those who fought for democracy, including the African National Congress supporters, there were the bombings in crowded areas, and the 'necklacing' murders in the townships, when tyres were put round the necks of supposed collaborators and then filled with petrol and set alight.

What is remarkable, when the history of the people under apartheid is taken in, is that the spirit of hope for something better than simple retributive justice did come to the fore in South Africa. The strength of the influence of the great spirits, Nelson Mandela, Desmond Tutu and others somehow made it possible for the climate of division, violence and hatred to be challenged and for an alternative way, a way of Africa and of community, of forgiveness and reconciliation, through the painful unearthing of the truth, to be open. Desmond Tutu called this way the way of restorative justice, which aims to heal and rehabilitate both victims and perpetrators, all children of God and all worthy of being restored. It is based on the understanding, raised by the Freedom Charter of the anti-apartheid liberation movement, that South Africa belongs to all the people who live in it.

The Truth and Reconciliation Commission was very representative of the people of South Africa, including Coloured,

Indian, African and white people. There were people from the political left and also from the right and there were Christians, a Muslim and a Hindu. The commission was greatly influenced by Christianity and by Christians, including those who had fought for the ending of apartheid. There were many famous figures who struggled to end apartheid, including Allan Boesak from the Dutch Reformed Mission Church, Frank Chikane, a General Secretary of the South African Council of Churches, Peter Storey, a head of the Methodist Church, Beyers Naude, an Afrikaaner and also a General Secretary of the South African Council of Churches and Denis Hurley, a Roman Catholic Archbishop of Durban.

It was significant that the new commission held its first meeting at Bishopscourt, the official home of Anglican archbishops of Cape Town and an important place of meeting for those who were working to end apartheid throughout the 1980s. This was the place from which the significant march of 1989 was planned, which began many demonstrations all over the country which were the trigger for the changes and freedom which quickly followed. This was the place Nelson Mandela went to for his first night of freedom on 11 February 1990. At the first meeting of the commission, on 16 December 1995, its chairperson, Desmond Tutu, suggested that its members should begin their work by going on a retreat to 'sharpen our sensitivities'. Near to the end of the commission's life and work its members went on retreat again, this time to visit the cells of the former inmates of Robben Island. The meetings of the commission all began and ended with prayer. Prayers were also held at midday, and when, in the Human Rights Violations Committee, the survivors told their stories, there were prayers, hymns and the lighting of candles. The world-wide Anglican Communion was alerted to the work of the commission and monks and nuns all over the world were asked to pray for all the people involved.

The Truth and Reconciliation Commission was established under the National Unity and Reconciliation Act. It had three committees. The committee on human rights violations offered the people who had suffered gross violations of their human rights the opportunity to tell their stories, which proved to be a healing process for many. The committee made the violations known and tried, often successfully, to find out who the perpetrators were and why the crimes had been committed. Many people who shared their stories, some at public hearings which were televised and broadcast all over the world, told Desmond Tutu that they felt a heavy load taken away from their shoulders.

The committee on amnesty offered the people who had committed the human rights abuses the opportunity to apply for amnesty. Amnesty was only possible if there was a political reason for the atrocities, committed between 1 March 1960, the date of the Sharpeville Massacre, and 10 May 1994, when elections were held and freedom came. This was not an excuse for any murderer to be exonerated of his or her crimes. The perpetrators of the crimes further had to confess everything they did. Applications for amnesty had to be in place by 10 May 1997.

The committee on reparations and rehabilitation worked to find out what harm the victims of the crimes and their families suffered and to provide support before, during and after the hearings. They also consulted the communities on the impact of the violations and on ways of achieving reparation and rehabilitation. This committee made recommendations to the President and to Parliament for immediately needed assistance and for more long-term assistance and measures to prevent further human rights abuses in the future. It was made clear that any assistance given could only be a token and that it could never be commensurate with the atrocity which had been suffered.

It was Desmond Tutu's hope, partly fulfilled, that the work of the commission would be a healing process, not just for those who took part, but for the whole nation.

A symbolic occasion, a sign of healing and hope for the

future of South Africa's children, took place when Desmond Tutu came to England not long after the 1994 elections in South Africa and unveiled a statue of a gaunt African carrying a dead child in his arms. The child represented all those who had been killed in the 1976 massacre of the children. The statue is a memorial to the dead and is in St Martin-in-the-Fields Church in Trafalgar Square in Central London. At the same time a living memorial, a trust fund for education, has also been launched by people of many cultures. People across the world have joined together to share in building the free South Africa.

Today in the early twenty-first century there are many problems in South Africa, including township violence and unemployment, but many of the people are growing in confidence and in their hopes for a good future. Khayelitsha for instance is not a new heaven on earth, but it is a place of hope and of faith in God. It covers a larger area of the very sandy Cape Flats than it used to, and the houses need constant sweeping to clear the fine sand from the floors. There are probably around a million people living in the town. The standard of properties varies; some have few facilities, perhaps electric light but no water. Many of the houses are little more than tiny tin huts crowded together, some may be without furniture, others are more spacious and well furnished. Every residence is home to a family and most of the homes are cared for with love. People in fact make the best of what they have, which is often very little even now; they just get on with their lives.

Ailsa Moore, a member of the Autumn 2001 Christians Aware group, stayed in a home where the family earned a little money by baking and selling cakes. She was very impressed by the people she met. She wrote,

> *We were made really comfortable, the beds looked lovely. There was no water in the house yet we were given hot water to wash with. The only toilets were outside and had*

no lights, we were escorted there and warned not to leave the house after dark and we were left buckets to use if needed. It was made clear to us that it was dangerous for us to venture out without an escort because we were not known; this situation has not changed over the years.[1]

Ailsa remembers going to the church, where everyone had come out looking smart and putting their hearts and souls into their worship. The children playing outside were happy and friendly. The visitors were entertained by singing, a band playing, children performing, excellent food and wonderful handicrafts to admire and buy. The people in Khayelitsha are making the most of their lives, as are many more people who are materially poor and living in the shanty towns of South Africa in the early twenty-first century.

The 'Tikkun' project is a powerful example of the post-apartheid flowering of the human spirit in ordinary people and in the most unlikely places. Jonathon Freedland has written about this work, 'a worldwide fraternity dedicated to nothing less than the transformation of modern life'.[2] The inspiration for the project is Michael Lerner, one time spiritual guru to Hillary Clinton. The goal of the community is *tikkun olam* – healing the world.[3] A visiting group from Christians Aware saw a play on this work, by teenagers from the Ntwasahlobo School in the Khayelitsha township in District Six in Cape Town. The play spoke of hope and strength. Mark Coleman, a member of the group, has written,

The star of the drama was a short young man who spoke with a big voice. A natural leader. We loved his passion. But the young people at that school spoke with one voice, across their own ethnic and cultural and gender divides, about the

---

1. Ailsa Moore's Report to Christians Aware, 2001.
2. Jonathon Freedland, the *Guardian*, 2 January, 2002.
3. More information about the community can be found at the web site www.tikkun.org.

problems that confronted their community. There were no easy solutions and real mourning for the cost of AIDS, but they spoke together – an example of a community tapping into that which can heal the world. Tikkun olam.

Mark and other members of the group remember that the young people, and their excellent youth workers, in this project funded by the Cape Town Jewish Community, dealt with real issues and demonstrated that problems could be faced and transformed into possibilities. In Khayelitsha the youth work involved enabling the teenagers to express the stories about AIDS, poverty, unemployment and education. Both are important and are about healing. The group was reminded that however serious the problem, it can be transformed by people working together. To work together – not disabled by difference – is surely itself an act of faith which may be one of the fruits of the work for truth, forgiveness and reconciliation. What is hoped for now is that the many small signs of hope may soon be welded into a national movement by all the people of South Africa, towards becoming one community. There is still enough division to make this very much a hope and dream for the future, but not an impossible one.

But many of the hopes of the people, for decent homes for everyone and a return of some of the land which was taken away from them over years of colonialism and apartheid, have still to be realised. The twentieth-century increase in shanty towns has not slowed down and the crime rate in them has gone up. Many of those who lived privileged lives before apartheid ended are still living the same lives. There is much that needs to be changed, towards more equality of living and education between the many groups of people, but also, and rather more importantly, change is still needed in the minds of too many, who are still set in an apartheid society of privilege and deprivation.

Neverthless, Desmond Tutu's hope of a society where people, through facing the truth and coming to forgive others, were reconciled, is there in the South Africa of today. The 2001 visiting group from Britain spoke about their wonderful experience in taking part in the Eucharist at St Michael and All Angels in Khayelitisha. This church has a life-size black Christ hanging high up in the sanctuary. A priest member of the group remembered,

> *The service was about three hours in length yet it was not boring or tiring. There were several factors which made the liturgy work its magic . . . concelebrating at St Michael and All Angels was a joy, because in the Eucharist was a sharing of real fellowship, symbolised in the English words I spoke and the Xhosa words spoken by the other priests . . . What was good about this service is that there was a real ownership, and an offering by the people in their joyful singing, their dancing, their wearing of uniforms, their investing in new orders . . . this was a place people were forcibly located to, on the basis of their ethnic background – this made this an experience to remember. Prayers of penitence had a different ring. Celebrating the Peace with our brothers and sisters of that community meant much more than politeness . . . Worship at St Michael and All Angels touched me deeply. It spoke of the liberation of God that is, and is to come.*[1]

In December 1999 a huge piece of waste land in the centre of District Six in Cape Town was chosen as the central point for a gathering of three thousand people of all the major world faiths from all over the world. This was the Parliament of the World's Religions. The procession to the stage setting in District Six was described by a participant.

> *I am walking with two or three thousand others in a procession from the initial gathering in the beautiful company gardens in the centre of Cape Town to the outskirts. Here*

---

1. Christians Aware Report.

are dog collars alongside turbans and flowing saffron robes and banners of all colours in a variety of languages. The gentle hum of Buddhist chanting mingles somehow harmoniously with that of the Hindu mantras and the Christian songs. We may not understand them all but there are smiles of recognition, the graciousness of acceptance of the other and a feeling of real fellowship and common purpose as we walk together.[1]

By hosting the Parliament of the World's Religions District Six was in some ways returning to its former and pre-apartheid glory as a rich multi-cultural and inter-faith community. This was made possible by some of the ordinary people who had lived there and who, when they themselves were moved away to the Cape Flats, had pleaded for the places of worship to be spared. Today these same places, including St Mark's Church, the Moravian Church and the mosque, are all thriving centres for worship. The people travel to them, because the destroyed homes have not been rebuilt. There is still the huge waste land but also now the technical university and an arena.

Some of the original inhabitants of District Six were there to meet the members of the Parliament of the World's Religions.

In October 2001 the visiting Christians Aware group attended an inter-faith peace service in the Claremont Road Mosque in the centre of Cape Town. The service was held following the 11 September 2001 atrocity and people of faith were anxious to:

Reach beyond our ghettos of piety. We need to be genuine and fearless as we meet as friends, and as co-workers for a peaceful world. We need to ensure that there is not a false dawn on the long road to freedom and to reach out beyond

---

1. *Parliament of the World's Religions*, Gwyneth Little, in the Easter 2000 *Christians Aware* magazine.

our conflicts. Those who sit around a table are less likely to look down the barrel of a gun, or engage in name-calling.[1]

It is very encouraging that in this gathering, of people of all faiths, there was the feeling that in politics, society and religion 'ubuntu' needs to be focused on. Only then can each person's humanity be recognised and only then can people look at each other and recognise that all are holy.[2] It was such an understanding that led the Christian champions of anti-apartheid and of the post-1994 movement for truth, forgiveness and reconciliation to make their sacrifices of life, commitment and hard work.

---

1. Christians Aware Report.
2. 'Ubuntu' is used in several Bantu languages, e.g. Zulu, Xhosa, Ndebele: To be human is to affirm one's humanity by recognising the humanity of others and, on that basis, establish respectful human relations with them.

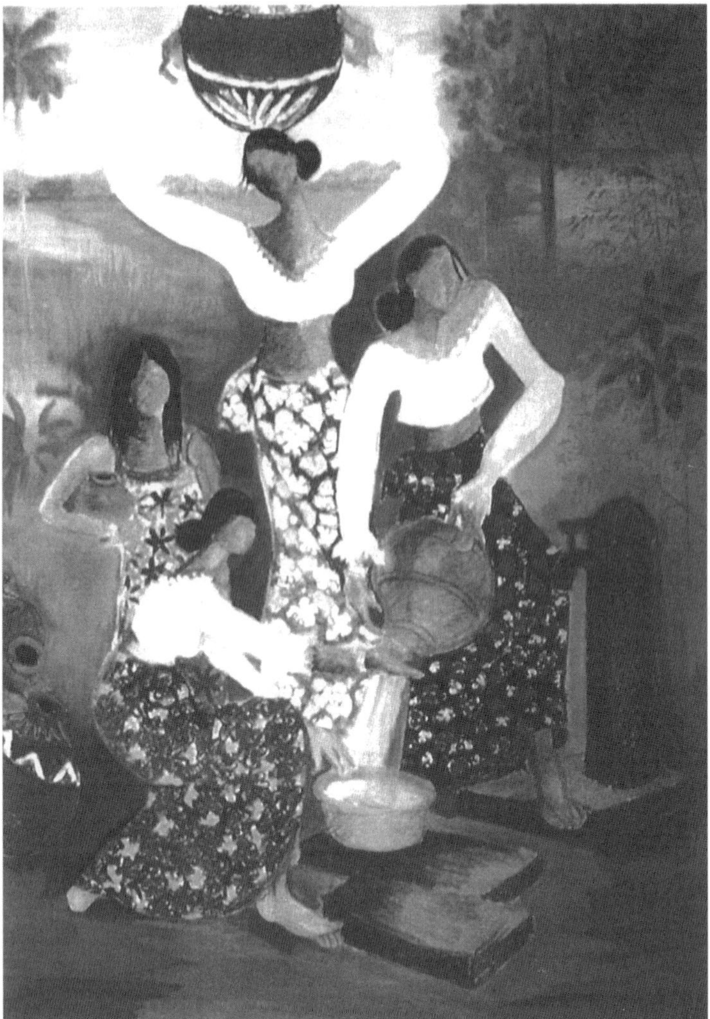

Water for Life in Tanzania

Now Jacob's well was there, Jesus therefore, being wearied with his journey, sat thus on the well . . . There cometh a woman of Samaria to draw water; Jesus saith unto her, 'Give me to drink.'
St John 4:6-7

Shamburai is a village near to Arusha which is reached by a dry and badly rutted road. There are three churches in the village, Lutheran, Pentecostal and Roman Catholic. Shamburai is in a very dry area and the people badly need water. A group from Christians Aware went out to build a much needed well in the Summer of 2000. The site was marked and equipment gathered together ready for the work to begin. There was one 'expert' and the rest of the workforce was of volunteers from Britain and from the Tanzanian churches, who took it in turns to join in. There was no power drilling equipment for this piece of work, but just the strength of the people, helped by a series of long interconnecting poles with a device on the end which served the dual purpose of digging and collecting samples of mud with which to test the nearness of water. The poles were surmounted by a crossbar which had to be pushed by the volunteers. They laboured for five days before the first muddy water was reached and after that it did not take long to reach the clear healthy water. This was very good news and the cause of great rejoicing and celebration, for now all the people of Shamburai are able to drink the water freely and safely.

Water covers more than 70 per cent of the Earth's surface, but only three per cent is freshwater. Until recently water was considered an endless resource, but in August 2002 the *Guardian* published a headline, 'Water – the issue of this century'.[1] During the twentieth century the quantity of water

---
1. The *Guardian*, August 22nd, 2002.

used in agriculture has increased tenfold while the world's wetlands are much reduced. It is estimated that over the next 30 years water use will go up by 50 per cent. At the same time more than 1 billion of the world's people do not have access to clean water. A further 1.7 billion people, some statistics give 3 billion, do not have access to adequate sanitation. The horror of the situation can be understood from one simple statistic: between 27,000 and 30,000 people die every day from diseases caught through drinking unhealthy water.[1] The horror is magnified when the estimate that half the world's population, in Africa, the Middle East and South Asia, will face severe water shortages by 2025 is taken in.[2]

The horror grows and comes home to those of us who live in the developed world when we remember that in 1992 the United Nations Earth Summit in Rio de Janeiro launched a great campaign to work for sustainable development. The hope was that the world would unite to tackle environmental problems and injustices, including pollution, the depletion of resources and declining biodiversity, and also the scandal of poverty, hunger, and the general inequality of living conditions for the world's people. Agenda 21 was the document which offered guidance on the way forward. The developed world was to increase its aid to the developing world, and the debts of the developing world were to be reduced. Neither hope has been fulfilled in a way which will make a difference. One of the recommendations of Agenda 21 was that the world would pull together to provide universal access to safe drinking water and sanitation. Can the world work to make sure that the same recommendations from the 2002 Earth Summit in Johannesburg will be more effective?

About four-fifths of preventable disease in the developing world is the result of people drinking contaminated water.[3]

---

1. Statistic from the World Health Organisation.
2. World Bank estimate.
3. Statistic from *New Scientist*, August 2002.

Most of the world's deadliest diseases are water borne, including cholera, amoebic dysentery, typhoid, hepatitis, all the diarrhoeal diseases, infections of the intestine, trachoma, scabies, leprosy, malaria, river blindness, yellow fever, schistosomiasis, dengue fever and elephantiasis. In fact it is probable that more than 80 per cent of the world's diseases stem from lack of safe water and adequate sanitation.[1] Some improvements have been made in the last ten years: the number of people dying from diarrhoea has fallen by 28 per cent and the number dying from measles has fallen by 26 per cent. However, there has been a 25 per cent increase in deaths from malaria to 1.8 million a year, and a sixfold leap in HIV related deaths to 3 million a year.

Water is not scarce in every area of Tanzania. The offshore islands and the coastal belt, where many people live, is a flat lowland along the shores of the Indian Ocean, with a tropical climate and heavy rainfall. Inland from the coast is the huge area of the central plateau which is very dry and very poor. Shamburai is a very small village in this huge area of the country. There are mountains to the north and their slopes are good for farming. This area includes Mount Kilimanjaro, famous as the highest mountain in Africa and a centre for mountaineers from all over the world. The Lake Victoria area has good rainfall and a heavy population. This is the plantation area of the country, with sisal and sugar cane.

The variety of the landscape in Tanzania is apparent to all its visitors, most of whom go to the coast, the mountain and the game parks. I have visited many game parks in this vast country. On one occasion I went to Lake Manyara to the West of Arusha with a group, travelling through a thousand shades of green forest to a sparkling hippo pool full of grunting animals. I also saw zebra, giraffe, elephant, wildebeeste, buffalo and impala, and returned to the camp to enjoy a delicious meal and a sound sleep. On every day of the visit I saw picture

---

1. World Health Organisation.

postcard views of animals against the beauty of lake, mountain and crater. Most non-Tanzanians see the country through the eyes of tourists, and have no time and perhaps little inclination to see through the eyes of the people who live there.

Tanzania is a stunning country when seen through the eyes of its visitors. Many of its own people see it a little differently. Those who live on the dusty central plateau live there throughout their short lives, travelling, often by foot, over the dusty and pot-hole ridden roads and paths which never see a tourist. They have to provide food and water for themselves and the children. In Tanzania children are 60 per cent of the population of over 30 million people. Sometimes it is easier to find food than to find clean water. In this country of contrasts, of beauty and of suffering, the infant death rate is high, with 144 children per 1000 dying before the age of five years. Malnutrition is normal, malaria is a killer, and following the world-wide trend, is on the increase. AIDS is added as the late twentieth-century scourge. I have focused on the AIDS pandemic in the chapter on Central Africa, looking especially at how it has affected Zambia and Malawi.

Tanzania is in a sad situation at the beginning of the twenty-first century as one of the poorest countries in the world. An Englishwoman who is married to a Tanzanian went to live in Arusha in 1998 and has written about her struggles in a town which is potentially very attractive, with Mount Mweru looming above it and flowers everywhere. However, the roads are un-repaired so that clouds of dust or mud are thrown up every time a car drives down a street, and it is a major expedition to travel from Arusha to Dodoma, the captial city, because the road is almost non-existent. Most people are so desperately poor that they stand on the streets and try to sell anything they can find, including, when there are cuts in the water supply, buckets of water. Sadly people increasingly turn to crime. The country which achieved independence in 1961 with so many hopes for a good future has been badly disappointed.

The United Republic of Tanzania was founded in 1963 under the leadership of President Julius Nyerere, a practising Roman Catholic, who had great visions for the future development of the people and the country, and who was elected for three terms of office before he retired in 1985. His special contribution to his country and to Africa in general, was the development of African Socialism. In 1967 his ruling party, the Tanzanian African Union, issued the Arusha Declaration proclaiming an egalitarian and self-sufficient socialist society based on cooperation in every aspect of life, and especially in farming. This was called 'ujamaa', a Swahili word meaning 'family-hood' or 'community'. The government introduced the collectivisation of the villages of the country, sometimes moving people to form new settlements which were more viable. This was unpopular and soon broke down however. Perhaps one lasting result was that people came to see themselves as 'Tanzanian' first, rather than as members of their particular tribes. The exception to this is the Maasai people, who proudly continue to keep their nomadic cattle-keeping culture intact. Julius Nyerere introduced mass literacy campaigns and established the free and universal education which was at first successful but which has not, due to the increasing poverty, continued.

The seeds of the present dire poverty of Tanzania were sown in the 1970s when, in 1978, an invasion by Idi Amin from Uganda was repelled and Idi Amin was overthrown. At the same time the economy of Tanzania was failing because the prices paid for the main exports, coffee, spices, cotton, pyrethrum and cashew nuts, were falling. The prices for imported goods were rising. In 1977 the East African Economic Community, of Kenya, Uganda and Tanzania was dissolved. In 1985 Julius Nyerere retired and Ali Hassan Mwinyi, who won the election, took over. The movement towards full democracy had begun. In 1986 an economic recovery plan was launched, including incentives for private investment, but this plan depended on many changes including the creation of private capital. The changes never really happened and efforts to bring them about have led to the failure of socialist development, the borrowing of money, the debt, the pledges of economic adjustment, part of which included the reduction of the education budget, and the current situation. There was an influx of refugees from the Rwandan crisis in 1994 but some of them were expelled in 1996 after President Mkapa was elected. In 1997 Tanzania was overtaken by floods, caused by the effects of El Nino, and the resulting damage brought famine and yet more disease. The production of cotton and coffee also fell, thus adding to the general poverty in a country where fewer tourists were attracted, even to the game parks and the coast.

I have visited the Tarangiri Game Park, which is bleaker than Lake Manyara so that the animals are easier to see even far into the distance. It is also more typical of the dry land of much of the central plateau. Minjingu is a village near to Tarangiri. In the mid-1990s it was selected by the Diocese of Mount Kilimanjaro to be the place of an experiment focusing on education, seed loan and clean water. Education has included instruction in child care, including the enabling of the local community to identify nutritional and other diseases; the building of pit latrines and well-ventilated houses. Family planning classes are open to men as well as women. Seed loan is accompanied by help to improve farming methods and has been so successful that production has increased from almost nothing to 15 bags of maize per acre over an area of 25 acres.

The 'three pot' system has been introduced to provide clean water. It is a simple system and can be taken up by any community in need of clean water, given a little support and the will to change. The system requires the use of three large earthenware pots. Water from the river is collected in one of the pots and allowed to rest for about 24 hours, so that the river mud settles to the bottom of the pot. The cleaner water is poured off into the second pot, and again the water is allowed to rest, so that impurities settle to the bottom of the pot. Finally the water is poured into the third pot and again allowed to rest. The water is poured from the third pot into pans, where it is boiled and drunk by the people.

The next stage of the project will be to sink wells so that clean water will be assured. There is now a health committee of women and men, and there are plans to help people in other villages to learn about and practise primary health care. Before the experiment began in Minjingu it was similar to most other villages in this area of Tanzania to the west of Arusha, with its people suffering from dysentry and cholera, and with about six children dying every month. This is no longer the case in Minjingu. The value of clean water for healthy living has been demonstrated by a church initiated project which will hopefully be taken up by many other villages.

The churches in Tanzania, of all denominations, have been involved in health care, along with education and evangelism, for as long as they have existed.

Roman Catholicism grew in the region following the journeys of Vasco da Gama at the end of the fifteenth century. As the Church grew its missioners became divided between those who embraced the local culture and traditions and those who felt that conversion to Christianity necessitated a move away from African roots. The report of the Second Vatican Council followed independence in many countries. Perhaps the most dramatic change which the Council brought in was the introduction of the vernacular liturgy. In the African context this heralded the use of tribal languages and African music and song and also a deeper journey into roots. The people felt at home in their Church, and gladly took up another challenge from the Second Vatican Council, of commitment to development in its widest and deepest sense. It had always included health care, and education, and now it included water engineering and farming. The people saw their mission as one to love and care for the whole person; body, mind and spirit.

The Lutheran Church followed German colonialism, but remained in place when Tanganyika became a British mandated territory at the end of World War One.

A focus on the whole person has always been the hope of Anglican missionaries to the region. The first were those who went out through the Universities Mission to Central Africa, which came into being following the famous 1857 appeal of David Livingstone to people in Britain to work in Africa. The UMCA soon realised that it was vital for the missionaries to train local African Christian leaders and in 1864 a training school with five freed slave boys was set up in Zanzibar. The training of girls followed in 1865. Soon the numbers of pupils grew and the indigenous church was begun. By the 1870s the school had a range of books in Swahili, including the Bible and Prayer Book, thanks to the efforts of the bishop, Edward Steere. In 1879 John Swedi was the first African to be ordained deacon.

Bishop Steere moved inland from Zanzibar and developed the mission station at Magila in the Usambara area. From there other mission stations were developed. There was also a mission at Ruvuma in the Masasi area in the south. The missions were run by ex-slave teachers, though English missioners were still 'in charge'. Schools were developed, including one at Magila, to teach some of the children of the area, who had never been slaves, and who would therefore be culturally closer to the people around them. I have been to Magila and experienced the grandeur, now dim and ghostly, which must, early in the twentieth century, have been real and solid.

Cecil Magaliwa was an important figure in the development of the church and people in Tanzania.[1] He was a freed slave who was educated at the church school in Zanzibar and

---

1. Cecil Magaliwa's life is included in *The Evolution of an African Ministry and the work of the UMCA in Tanzania. 1864-1909*, J. T. Moriyama, 1984, PhD thesis, London.

became a teacher in 1878 and then a reader. He married another ex-slave, Lucy Magombeani. Cecil was very bright and in 1883 he was sent to England, to St Augustine's College in Canterbury. On his return home in 1886 he was made a deacon and went to Chitangali Mission, first alone, and later to settle with Lucy and their children. He learnt the local language, Yao, developed the school and had the support of the chief of the whole area. He was made a priest in 1890 and was known far and wide as a wise and brave person, on one occasion dealing with a rumoured attack by the Ngoni people by sending everyone away to the hills while himself remaining behind. He had a clear vision for the self reliance of the African Church, and always built new churches solely from the offerings and free labour of the people. At the same time he never lost his contacts with friends made when he was in England and was not shy to ask them for funds for the school, especially for teaching materials.

He made the first Christian converts among the Makonde people, placed teachers and built schools. By 1893 Chitangali was the Christian centre of a huge area and Cecil Magaliwa moved around all of it. At the same time other African priests emerged. Sadly Cecil Magaliwa retired to Zanzibar in 1897 partly because the chief, now an agent for the German colonial government, would no longer support him, and partly because he began to sense some hostility from local people when he tried to establish new missions. One sign of this was a robbery to the family home. After this African ministry was not developed as it should have been, and European missioners were 'in charge' until the 1905 Maji – maji rising, when the Europeans withdrew for a while and the Africans stood alone. However, Europeans always remained in the most senior posts in the churches, until after the independence of the country.

An African man who rose to leadership in his own diocese and then in his country, as the Anglican Archbishop of Tanzania, was, like his grandfather Cecil Magaliwa, born and brought up on the island of Zanzibar, and trained and employed as a teacher before seeking ordination. Archbishop John Ramadhani was ordained as a priest in 1976 in the great cathedral built by Edward Steere on the site of the old slave market on Zanzibar. He was ordained as a bishop in 1980 and became Archbishop of Tanzania in 1984, when he had opportunities to visit England, including Canterbury, the place his grandfather had appreciated so much. He is now retired and living again on his beloved Zanzibar island. As Bishop of Tanga and Zanzibar John Ramadhani truly followed in his grandfather's footsteps by living with the people, always in a small and simple home, and by working with them for the development of every aspect of their lives. He has initiated the building of many churches and has encouraged the Christians to give their labour freely towards the building. He has enabled the development of many new congregations, and he has also developed education and the health of the people, always having great love and respect for them, including those who are Muslims.

I have taken part in camps in the Diocese of Zanzibar and Tanga, including one when English and local volunteers joined together to dig an irrigation channel down from the mountains and into a village on the edge of the hillside, where a huge hole in the ground was prepared. I was there when the life-giving water from the mountains was allowed to break through into the huge hole, or fish tank, to provide much needed food for the people. The bishop and village people were not content with one fish tank, this was a pioneering venture, which was then spread to other villages and people to help them to fight the poverty which has afflicted and afflicts most of the people of the country.

Christians have worked over the years to try to remove injustices which come with dire poverty and to offer facilities which make a full life possible. They have had some success in this work. Minjingu is not an isolated village which has worked with the churches to achieve a better quality of life for the people. However, there have always been and still are many problems, not least the isolation of large numbers of the people, who live in a small and harsh world of their own, often unaware of the churches and the nation they are living in. Lack of training in planning and organisation is a huge problem for many people, and something the churches are struggling to work on. It is said that about 70 per cent of the people can now read and write, but this figure is questioned, and in recent years it may have declined. Only 6 per cent of boys and 5 per cent of girls achieve secondary education.[1]

Christians are 48 per cent of the population in Tanzania today, Muslims are 32 per cent, leaving 20 per cent of people who follow traditional African religions. The largest Christian group is the Roman Catholic group, followed by Lutherans and Pentecostals.

The Anglican Church is a small but very significant minority among the Christians. Today the Christian Council of Tanzania and the Tanzanian Episcopal Committee are important bodies, working together on education and social issues.

In recent years the commitment to education and health care has been increased, because the once hoped for government provision has not been as all-embracing as was envisaged. The churches in Tanzania have developed and are running at least 50 per cent of the health institutions of the country. They provide at least 55 per cent of the health services. The Kilimanjaro Medical Centre, run by the churches, was opened in 1971 and offers an excellent service and many learning opportunities not just within Tanzania but for the whole of East Africa. Primary health education and care are at the centre of its programme and concern. This is a people centred and holistic approach to health care which encourages the people and the communities to organise themselves around health issues and to understand and tackle the

---

1. Statistics for literacy and secondary school attendance are for 1995, from the United Nations Population Division.

underlying and root causes of ill health and death. Workers from the Kilimanjaro Centre go out to the villages to teach people about the essentials of preventative health care, including the need for clean water and sanitation together with agriculture and nutrition, education and community development.

The Anglican Church of the Province of Tanzania has a huge share in the health education and provision for the people of the country. The Provincial Development Office was established in 1988 and has an officer and a development advisory group which includes outside bodies, churches and groups. The direct target group for the development programme is senior staff in the dioceses around the country. Many training programmes are now organised, through the 'Human Resource Development Programme', so that those who are trained in health care and education may in their turn train others. There is also a small fund, the enabling fund, which is given to encourage small community projects. The focus is put on education, so that people can actually know why they should work for health, through working for clean water and adequate sanitation and nutrition. The main groups of people focused on by the development officer and his team are women and especially those with young children under the age of five years, the unemployed young people in both the rural and urban areas, disabled people and the small farmers and pastoralists.

It was not surprising to me that I was taken with one of my groups to a remote area to the west of Arusha, to meet people in all the groups focused on by the church, women and young children, unemployed young people, disabled people and the farmers and pastoralists. We drove by bus for several hours to Lake Langata, to meet the people, most of whom seemed to be children, who were not only living in thick dust but were themselves covered in it. We were taken on a tour of the village, into homes, into the primary school and the very unfinished secondary school, and into the windowless wooden church for songs and prayers. Finally we were asked to sit down in the wooden meeting place to eat the lunch which was offered. When the food came it was one of the most delicious meals I have ever tasted, of simple home-made bread, and fish from the lake. The decision of the church pioneers and of those who followed them, to share and work with the people and to enable them to go on to do more was surely the wisest decision they made. We were fortunate to share with the people of Lake Langata.

It is not surprising to me that I am often asked to send groups to work at the development of schemes to provide clean water for the people in Tanzania. Shamburai was one such project. The fish tank and irrigation channel in the Usumbara Hills was another project. In 1998 a group went to Iborou, the home of Maasai people who have settled on the edge of Arusha, where there has always been a shortage of water. A clean water tank was built and mounted on an 8-foot high concrete block cross piece. An existing borehole was used to pump the water through a pipeline and into the tank. A tap was fitted at the bottom of the tank, with a small enclosure around the tank. The tank will always be kept full of water and used for storage, ready for the many times when there is no water in the pipeline.

Another 1998 group worked at the water supply for Munguishi, the centre for lay training in the Diocese of Mount Kilimanjaro. This work included the damming of a stream and the building of a pumping station. The dam was built in a natural basin in the stream, with hardcore in the bottom of the stream and concrete laid over it. The walls of the basin were then lined, a pipeline was laid and a sluice gate built at the front of the dam to control the water level. The training centre and local community now have a continuous supply of water.

The Munguishi Training Centre trains lay people for a holistic ministry. Teaching people all over a huge area of the Diocese of Mount Kilimanjaro about primary health care, including the need for clean water, is life-giving now and for the future. It is one small symbol of what is possible for the whole of Tanzania.

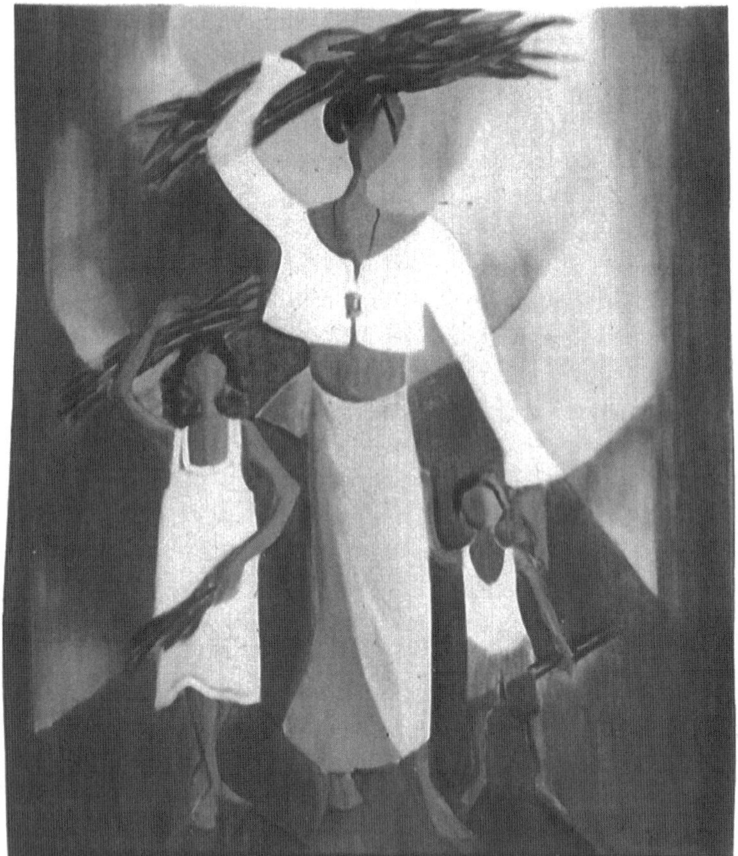

Moving and Growing in Kenya

They that wait upon the Lord will renew their strength; they shall mount up with wings as eagles; they shall run and not be weary; and they shall walk and not faint.
                                              Isaiah 40:31

In August 1994 three groups, from Nyeri, Mumias and Rabai, set off to walk to Nairobi to mark the 150th anniversary celebrations of the Anglican Church of the Province of Kenya. They were re-living some of the history of the ACK, including the journey made by Dr Krapf from Rabai and the journey of William Jones to take the news of Bishop Hannington's death to Mombasa. The walkers included a cross section of Kenyan society, teachers, a policeman, evangelists, an engineer, students, clergy, bishops and many others. Wurtemberg, the area of Germany the Krapfs came from, was represented by a specially invited group.

The Nyeri group was led by Bishop Alfred Chipman, first bishop of the Diocese of Mount Kenya West, which was formed in 1994 from the Diocese of Mount Kenya Central. The members of the Nyeri Group preached in the open air and at churches along the way of the anniversary walk. The Diocese of Mount Kenya West has its cathedral in Nyeri, a small market town situated on the plateau between the Abedare Mountains and Mount Kenya, the legendary home of Ngai, God of the Kikuyu people.

When the new diocese was formed I was invited to take a Christians Aware group to visit and share in a work camp in Dol Dol in the semi-desert region of Mukogodo. The visit and camp took place in 1995. Kenyan and British people together spent eight days building a dormitory for girls who would be the students at the church-run technical college. The work camp, in a Maasai area, with British and Kikuyu people on the work team, was symbolic of one of the main aims of the new diocese, to bring the Maasai and Kikuyu people together. The honey project is also a way of uniting the peoples. The cacti and trees of the drylands provide a superb environment for honey. The Maasai people make the wooden hives and hang them in the trees. The Kikuyu people buy the honey once it has been refined. The church enables the refining and also the marketing of the honey. The Maasai people use the 'honey money' to send their children to school and to supplement their diet.

Many other workcamps have taken place since 1995 including the building of the first stage of St Philip's Music School in Naro Moru, a place with a lovely stone built church on the edge of Mount Kenya, famous because Princess Elizabeth worshipped there just before she became Queen of the United Kingdom and the Commonwealth in 1952. A rainwater harvesting project was later developed in the Mukogodo area. A dam wall was built round a large area and the whole dam lined with stones and concrete. Then a pipe was laid from the dam to the cattle trough and the project presented to the local people. Another water harvesting project has been developed in the Abedare Mountains. In 1999 a Mukogodo ten-day camp put in pipes from the Kimanjo borehole to Oloborsoit, where water was very badly needed.

Today every Kenyan diocese has a diocesan missionary association, which works in the areas of outreach, evangelism and development. Christian mission was understood as much more than evangelism from the time of the early missionaries, who gladly took on the challenges of education, agriculture, community and health development, and even politics, as their own. These challenges have continued to have high priority for the Kenyan Church, and its members have accepted the unpopularity which has sometimes come their way without bitterness. The Church pioneered family planning in the early 1980s, when it was very unpopular with many people and when the normal family could be as many as nine or ten children. In the early twenty-first century the average

Kenyan family, certainly among those with secondary education, is likely to be of between two and four children and there are even young couples who look forward to a family of one or two children.

The 1994 anniversary walkers covered about 40 kilometres every day, and those of us who are regular walkers know how demanding this must have been. The fact that they wore through several pairs of shoes each and often had very sore feet are small indications of the rigours of the journey. They were true pilgrims, walking without knowing where they would spend the nights and depending upon the hospitality of the local people along their path.

The Kenyan Anglican Church, which, at the beginning of the twenty-first century, has grown to a membership of over two million in a country with over 17 million people, began when Mary and Johann Ludwig Krapf arrived in Mombassa from Zanzibar in 1844. They were pilgrims who had already suffered on their long journeys. They brought with them the commendation of Said Sultan, the Muslim ruler who was happy to support their work of telling the people about God. They arrived in a place which had no practising Christians, though there had been Roman Catholic Christians following the journeys of Vasco da Gama towards the end of the fifteenth century. Mary Krapf died in childbirth soon after her arrival in Mombasa. Her husband was also ill, but stoically went on to work for a base for the church, first at Rabai and then farther inland, helped by a Muslim trader and Johannes Rebmann, like himself a Church Missionary Society member, who joined him in 1846. The early pioneer missionaries were brave pilgrims who knew that they had a very good chance of dying on the journey. They had no regular contact with their home countries and missions and relied on local people every step of the way. It is heartening that Said Sultan, Muslim scholars and many local Muslims gave encouragement and support.

It is also heartening that in very recent years the Kenyan Church has made great efforts to enter dialogue with Muslims, seeking to understand and respect their missionary faith. The church has moved a long way from the days when its members from the inland areas would rarely meet or speak to a Muslim. Increased mobility for Christians and Muslims alike has meant that there is now much more meeting and sharing. Visits to the UK by members of the ACK over a period of more than twenty years have also meant that they have been introduced to people of many faiths and have taken their positive experiences home with them. A college for the study of Islam has now been set up in Kenya and opportunities for formal dialogue are regularly sought.

In a history of ACK we read: 'We must see our Muslim brothers and sisters also as human beings engaged in the same eternal search. We must seek to create understanding through dialogue'.[1]

The early European missionaries worked very hard to learn Swahili and other local languages. They prepared grammars, dictionaries and New Testament translations. They lived in African style homes and ate the local food. They involved the local people in their work from the beginning, so that much of the evangelisation was accomplished, largely through story telling and conversation, by the African people themselves. A few men and boys became Christian first, accepting biblical names, but never losing their African names. Today there is a new preference by some church members to have their children baptised with traditional African names.

The issue of how much traditional culture should be interfered with is still a central concern for the ACK, for most other Christians in Kenya and of course for Christians elsewhere in Africa.

The early missionaries do not seem to have interfered with some of the local customs very much. They accepted the

---

1. *Rabbai to Mummias. A Short History of the Church of the Province of Kenya. 1844-1944*, Uzima, 1994, p. 177.

drinking of the local palm wine but warned against excessive drinking. The church today does not accept the drinking of alcohol or of smoking by its members, but this puritanical approach perhaps came from the influence of the East African Revival Movement rather than from the European missionaries. It is generally felt that Christians should show a good example to those who are not members and who sometimes, or often, smoke and drink to excess and ruin their families.

In the early years the church seems to have accepted the tradition of circumcision for men and for women. Circumcision of women was later condemned by missionaries in some regions of Kenya and has largely died out in those areas. It was not condemned in other regions where it is still practised by many. When David Gitari who has recently retired as the Archbishop of Kenya, was asked which aspects of culture he felt the church should eradicate, which could be lived with and which should be embraced, he replied that female circumcision could be lived with, while cattle rustling should not. Many people, myself included, would disagree with this. It is hard for some of us who are not Africans to appreciate that male and female circumcision have been seen as marks of membership, of the clan, tribe, and even of the nation at the time of the struggle for independence.

Many Christians in Kenya did not support the Mau Mau movement for the independence of the country, which caused the state of emergency to be declared by the government between 1952 and 1960. Some African people were in fact killed for refusing to join the Mau Mau. Samuel Muhoro was an Anglican priest who was beaten and left for dead when he refused to take the oath. It was very moving to hear him tell his story in the chapel of twentieth-century Martyrs in Canterbury Cathedral a few years before he died. During the emergency some Christians acted as go-betweens and tried to bring reconciliation between members of the Mau Mau and members of the army. In some ways the Church led the way to independence, because by the 1950s it had many African clergy, while there were still very few African leaders in secular life. The emergency ended in 1960 and in 1961 the elections were held which made Jomo Kenyatta the first president of the country. Internal self-government came in 1963 with a new flag, national anthem and spirit. In 1964 Kenya became a republic and gradually one party rule was established.

1960 saw the creation of the Province of East Africa, of Kenya and Tanzania, with Leonard Beecher as the Archbishop. Many Church institutions now taken for granted, like the Mothers' Union, were introduced at this time. The first Diocesan Missionary Associations were founded in Nakuru and Mount Kenya Dioceses in 1962. The Church also made a determined effort to play its part in national life, something it has done bravely ever since.

The early missionaries spoke strongly against the slave trade and slavery and against the killing of twins or other babies which were not thought 'normal,' but even in 1978, when a Gabbra woman gave birth to twins, the newly ordained Anglican priest and his Roman Catholic colleague had a hard struggle to make sure that they lived. The Anglican priest and his wife Helen also brought up a baby girl born outside marriage when she should traditionally have been made an outcaste from her people.

The newly ordained priest to the Gabbra was Andrew Adano, ordained in 1976 and furnished with a camel, a mule and 40 goats for his ministry to his own northern nomadic people.[1] His ministry was one of constant movement in an area where there were no roads or even pathways. At first he walked around the area, from one settlement or 'manyatta' to the next, carrying a huge jerry can of water. Later, he took his tent and animals with him, and lived with the people, joining

---

1. *The Gospel on a Camel's Back. The Story of Andrew Adano Tuye*, John Mwenda, National Council of Churches of Kenya, 1998.

in conversation with them on an equal footing, sharing the good news of Jesus Christ with them and then leaving them to discuss their future commitment. The work of the Roman Catholic missioner, Vincent Donovan, was in some ways similar in approach.[1] Vincent Donovan baptised communities of people, when the whole community was ready for this to happen, thus fitting in with the tradition and culture of the Maasai people he worked with. Andrew Adano, however, took a different approach and taught that individual commitment was necessary.

Andrew's ministry was always linked to the living conditions of the people he worked with, and especially after his time for study and reflection in Britain and Canada. He never separated spirituality from practical work with the people. He helped with water projects, supplied relief food during famines and built schools. He was made the Assistant Bishop of Kirinyaga in 1993. The Church had high hopes for him as a future leader, but he died in a helicopter crash in 1996. As bishop he became a reconciler between warring factions among the tribes, always helping them to see the other side of an issue. He worked hard to move the Anglicans in the more prosperous parts of Kenya towards an understanding of the Gabbra people. There was a tendency to write off the Gabbra culture as un-Christian, but he saw it as moral, including their belief in God which was not always recognised by outsiders to the tribe. He taught that when the people became Christian they did not need to reject everything in their traditional culture, but rather to experience the enrichment of Christianity in their on-going lives.

One interesting link he made between the traditions of the people and Christianity was in his teaching on sacrifice. He pointed out that the people were used to the sacrifice of animals to please God, who would then give peace, rain and

---

1. *Christianity Rediscovered. The Epistle from the Maasai*, Vincent Donovan, SCM Press.

general stability. He realised that no matter how much the early Protestant missionaries tried to get rid of this practice they would always fail, as he himself failed, because loyalty to the tribe and its customs was stronger than death, even for practising Christians. He never joined in the sacrifices but said that they were 'tolerable,' and could be compared with the sacrifices the people make to send their children to school. He then went on to talk about the sacrifice of Jesus Christ and to suggest that the greatest sacrifice for any person is to do the will of God.

In his recognition of the godliness of some traditional culture Andrew Adano was ahead of most people in his Church. It is encouraging that the Anglican Church in Kenya has recently recognised his approach and that traditional religions are not rejected simply because they are traditional, but are acknowledged and also studied in the theological colleges. Christians are able to affirm their traditional roots and to take wing as Christians without being cut off from their history and from their ancestors.

When the new liturgy for the Eucharist was published in 1989 great efforts were made for it to reflect the traditions of the people. The introduction to the service, written by Bishop David Gitari, points out:

It is both thoroughly Biblical and authentically African. Let us enjoy worshipping the God of our fathers, through Jesus Christ his Son, in the power of the Holy Spirit.[1]

Muranga Cathedral in the Diocese of Mount Kenya Central has a series of murals on the life of Christ seen through the Kikuyu culture on its northern aisle wall. The mural of the nativity shows three wise women going to attend the birth of the Christ child, because a man would never attend a birth in Kikuyu culture. The picture is set in the time of the Mau

---

1. *A Modern Service of Holy Communion*, Uzima, 1989.

Mau emergency in Kenya, in the 1950s, and the women are walking through a dangerous bush area from one fenced area to another. In the second mural Jesus is being baptised in the tradition of the Kikuyu initiation ceremony. The mural of the last supper is of a Kikuyu meal in a traditional rondavel. The final mural is of the crucifixion of a Kikuyu Christ.

The affirmation by the Anglican Church in Kenya of the traditional cultural and religious roots of the people was nowhere more important and perhaps more surprising than in the area of polygamy. The tradition of the Anglican Church was that polygamists should not be baptised until they became monogamous. The development of a tradition of theological conferences for the Province of Kenya grew in the 1970s, and in the 1981 conference, which was held in Mombasa, polygamy was discussed and there were some who thought that the church could accept polygamists. At the 1988 Lambeth Conference in Canterbury, Bishop David Gitari spoke and proposed a change in church discipline for polygamists. The conference resolved:

This conference upholds monogamy as God's plan, and as the ideal relationship of love between husband and wife; neverthleless recommends that a polygamist who responds to the Gospel and wishes to join the Anglican Church may be baptised and confirmed with his believing wives and children on the following conditions:

- *that the polygamist shall promise not to marry again as long as any of his wives at the time of his conversion are alive*

- *that the receiving of such a polygamist has the consent of the local Anglican community*

- *that such a polygamist shall not be compelled to put away any of his wives on account of the social deprivation they would suffer*

- *and recommends that provinces where churches face problems of polygamy are encouraged to share information of their pastoral approach to Christians who become polygamists so that the most appropriate way of disciplining and pastoring them can be found...*[1]

The Church in Kenya has put this resolution into practice and the general feeling is that it has strengthened the Church's ministry.

Some people find it surprising that many of the African Christians were able to move to the acceptance of polygamists, on the condition they did not take more wives after their baptisms. This was a move away from the traditions of the Church and towards the older traditions of the people. It was more surprising than it might have been because many of the roots of the Kenyan Church are in the East African Revival Movement. This movement started in Rwanda in the 1920s and focussed on the cross and on personal repentance for sin, on personal salvation, Christian fellowship, evangelism and rejoicing in the Holy Spirit in worship. In Kenya the revival movement gained the ascendancy in the 1950s and 60s, and the tradition grew of huge revival meetings, led by the laity, following church services. Teaching was puritanical and centred on the family, of father, mother and the children. Perhaps the move towards the acceptance of polygamous relationships which existed before the members became Christian is an indication of the move of many Kenyan Anglican Christians away from the Revival Movement towards a much more open and tolerant Christianity.

Kenyan Anglicans have not moved in their attitudes to practising homosexual Christians, and have rejected the possibility that the position of practising homosexuals is compatible with the gospel. I have taken part in conferences when a cross section of African people were present, including

---

1. Lambeth Resolution, 1988.

young people, and found a very negative response to homosexuality. This was also true of the position of the African bishops at the Lambeth Conference in 1998. The only possibility for practising homosexuals, according to most African Christians, is for them to stop practising. One of the reasons for this immobility may be the important place the family, polygamous or monogamous, has in both traditional and more recent African culture. The first and most important reason for marriage, in traditional Christian teaching and in African culture, is the production of children. A Kenyan priest said to me recently, 'It is because I have children that I have a future'. Homosexuality is rejected by many African Christians because it is not allowed in the Bible, but perhaps also because it is not part of traditional culture, it has no purpose or long term value in a traditional African sense of values, and it is therefore not understood.

The Anglican Church in Kenya has moved a long way in its support for women in leadership in the Church including the ordained ministry. Andrew Adano was ahead of most Anglicans in Kenya in having no objections to women's ordination. He encouraged women to be trained for leadership in the church and community. He supported Naomi Waqo in her vocation to ministry. She went on to study theology at St Andrew's College and is the first woman priest in northern Kenya.

The Church in the Province of Kenya approved the ordination of women in June 1990 and the first three women were ordained in Kirinyaga in 1992. Women's ordination is now normal in many Kenyan dioceses. The rapid growth in the number of women priests in Kenya today is due in no small measure to the work of the Church Army, which trained sisters over a long period so that when the time was right they were ready to serve. Some friends who were Church Army sisters are now priests. It is encouraging that many Kenyan Anglican Christians have changed their attitudes to women in leadership positions in the church, and now encourage it where only a few years ago they were hesitant or against it. This change in thinking has happened together with a change in the attitudes of Kenyan Christians to women in society over the last ten years. At a recent gathering in Britain it was inspiring to hear young Anglican male priests recognising the vocations of women and supporting women's ministry.

The ordination of women in Kenya and women's general development is due in no small measure to David Gitari, the Archbishop of Kenya between 1996 and 2002. David Gitari's ministry began when he was a child in a Christian family on the slopes of Mount Kenya and will not end with his retirement in 2002. He has always seen life as a whole, his life as a Christian in Kenya, and his ministry, of evangelism and the development of every aspect of people's lives. He became famous when he was Bishop of Mount Kenya East for his travelling, his preaching and teaching, and his practice of celebrating the Eucharist and then changing the altar into a table for the discussion of the development needs of the people.

David Gitari told me of the impact on his life of the Lausanne Conference on World Evangelisation which took place in 1974. He became convinced then that it is impossible to care about people's souls and not about their bodies and minds. He became totally committed at that moment in time to work for justice and development alongside evangelism. He set up his diocesan board of Christian Community Services in 1978, which related to every aspect of life. A new venture was the introduction of mobile health clinics and the family planning programmes. In 1994 AIDS awareness was introduced. Another new venture was the setting up of six demonstration farms.

The church in Mount Kenya East grew rapidly with David Gitari as bishop. When the diocese started in 1975, there were 19 parishes and 150 congregations. Only 15 years later there were 93 parishes and 400 congregations and it was at this time that the diocese was divided into the dioceses of Kirinyaga and Embu. It was normal for David Gitari to confirm between 300 and 600 people every Sunday and he remembers one occasion when he was presented with 895 candidates so that he had to organise a tea break in the middle of the service. The growth of the church in the Mount Kenya East area was typical of the rest of the province, where new congregations were and are springing up all the time.

David Gitari has been a pioneer in the church in Kenya for high standards in the schools run by church, and many new primary and secondary schools have been built. He has also pioneered good theological education for the ordinands and clergy. He always sought young and well educated people for the church who would happily enter a three-year theological course before they were ordained. The other bishops of the province did not all agree with this approach. Bishop Sospeter Magua was Bishop of Mount Kenya South. He was keen to train people who had been part of the East African Revival Movement by giving them short courses before ordination. He saw this as the way to meet the growing demand for priests. More recently Alfred Chipman, Bishop of the new Diocese of Mount Kenya West, has ordained people after giving them very little training on the grounds that they were people who had been members of the church for a long time and who were loving and open in their on-going lives.

David Gitari started a new college at Kabare, the St Andrew College of Theology and Development. This was on a beautiful site, with a view of Mount Kenya and in the place where the first Church Missionary Society missionaries in this area had established a station in 1910. The college was opened in 1977 and a new library was built in 1991. Students come to the college from many countries, and some study for degrees.

David Gitari has been a brave challenger of government in Kenya, often preaching sermons against casual attitudes and lack of care for the people.[1] He challenged the system

---

1. *Let the bishop speak*, David Gitari, Uzima, 1988. *In Season and out of Season, Sermons to a nation*, David Gitari, Regnum, 1996.

which was introduced for people to vote for councillors and members of the national assembly by standing behind them, and he persisted for several years until the system was dropped. He became so unpopular with some people that in April 1989 his house was attacked and he and his family had to escape by climbing up onto the roof.

Another challenger to the government in Kenya today is Wangaari Maathai, the inspirer and leader of the Greenbelt Movement and a former Professor of Anatomy at the University of Nairobi. She sees her work as work to save Kenya from the danger of desertification due to the cutting down of the trees and the misuse of the land, and has often been very brave in resisting government opposition to her work. The Greenbelt Movement is dedicated to the planting of trees everywhere possible, as a symbol of hope and for the sake of the future of the country. It has a concern for the prevention of soil erosion, for food production and women's development, for self-employment of many of the people, for the future preservation of the indigenous trees and shrubs and for community activity and development. This movement is a grass-roots movement of tree planting by the people of Kenya and it has become great through the dedication of the National Council of Women of Kenya. The first tree-planting ceremony took place in June 1977 and following that the national campaign was launched, seeds distributed, nurseries begun and many millions of trees planted.

One important outcome of the Greenbelt Movement has been the jobs offered to hundreds of people, in both the urban and rural areas. School children have also been involved in the creation of public green belts.

The Greenbelt Movement is an independent organisation which is wholeheartedly supported by the churches of Kenya. There are church tours of the forests, church seed nurseries and special tree-planting ceremonies. The Diocese of Mount Kenya South has made a special excursion to the forests in April for the last two years, with Professor Maathai.

Every parish in the diocese is dedicated to plant trees every year.

I have taken part in tree planting with Kenyan Christians. We were introduced to the trees by a man who knew the uses of all of them, whether they were for barriers or shade, for fruits or for berries. He approached the trees with care and even love, realising that their growth is one of the keys to a good future for all the people. He, an ordinary Kenyan with very little education, is typical of many of the Christians in his country who are not afraid to move into new ways of thinking, working and growing for the future.

ASIA

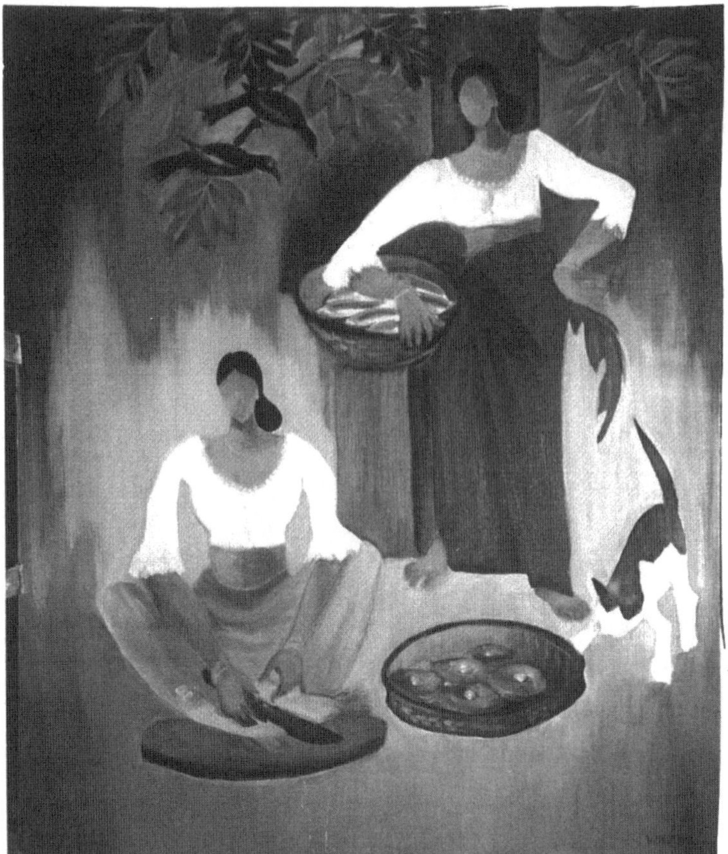

Solidarity and Sharing in Sri Lanka

Out of the depths have I cried to Thee, O Lord.
Lord hear my voice:
let thine ears be attentive
to the voice of my supplications.
If Thou, Lord shouldest mark iniquities,
Lord, who shall stand?
But there is forgiveness with Thee.
                              Psalm 130:1-4

Looking from this garden I see God
smiling in the gold of fields
stooked harvest square.

But what of the harvest of hate
and anguished dread, the scarred and dead
whose lives and homes are burnt
as one burns spurned stubble:
in the field, the house, the street
where they have fallen on the ground
like seeds, what will be reaped?

O what a bitter wound within the nation,
what black hurricanes of desolation.
Why such awful vengeance?
When we cry out does God answer
only by his silence?
Or is his answer in the brave, just, kind
who serve the plight of fugitives,
not hiding from stark truth and grief
but seeking how to heal and bind
the sundered in one sheaf?[1]

---

1. Olive Hitchcock's poem is included in *Out of the Depths. Struggle and Hope in Sri Lanka*, Christians Aware, 1992.

This poem was written by Olive Hitchcock in 1983 but it is still relevant in the Sri Lanka of today. It conveys the stark contrast which exists between the beauty of the land and the suffering of the people. A recent visitor wrote on her return home, 'Sri Lanka to me is a country of two halves. One half is beautiful, friendly, and seeking peace between faiths and ethnic groups, the other half is of death, fear, conflict and loss'.[1]

Sri Lanka is an extremely beautiful country, of magnificent mountains, hills, plains and coastlines. Until the middle and late twentieth century when troubles boiled up and spluttered out to scar every person who lives there, it was a famous destination for the world's tourists, many of whom went to sit on the beaches and to see the fishing communities living and working there. Visitors have always admired Sri Lanka's natural beauty and also the wonders of the civilisation created by its people over the centuries. Much of Sri Lanka is dry, and therefore the people built what has become a famous network of irrigation canals and reservoirs or tanks. Many of the ancient canals and tanks have been restored and some of them are in temple precincts. The temples and monasteries in well known and little known places are unique in the world. I have visited Anuradhapura, one of the famous pilgrim places, which is full of temples, palaces and statues, including a world famous one of the seated Buddha. I have also visited temples which are unknown. One of these was out in the drylands of the northern part of the island. Its setting was superb and its reclining stone Buddhas were breathtaking.

Sri Lanka is full of bald contrasts, from one place to another, from one people to another and even from one moment to another. This climate was quite shocking until very recently for all those who live in Sri Lanka, though the 2002 declarations of commitment to peace by the Liberation Tigers of Tamil Eelam have given a hope to cling on to for

---

1. Carol Gotham who visited Sri Lanka with Christians Aware in 2000.

many people. The Agreement on a Ceasefire was signed between the Government of Sri Lanka and the LTTE on 22 February 2002. The peace talks between the government and the Tamil Tigers began in Thailand in September 2002. It is now safe to walk around in the South and in Colombo, and people's hopes are therefore high. However, this is only a beginning of the peace process and many problems must be solved. There is hardly a family anywhere in the country that has escaped bereavement. Many people are traumatised, many are suffering from mental illness and for a few the ethos of violence has encouraged violent behaviour in the communities and homes, which does not stop when there is a new public commitment to peace.

In Sri Lanka at the beginning of the twenty-first century there is hope of peace but it still feels possible to be surrounded by beauty, feeling secure and hopeful one minute, and for it all to be dashed and destroyed the next. Michael Ondatje, in his novel set in Sri Lanka, *Anil's Ghost*, conveys the contrasts wonderfully. His descriptions of this stunning country are vivid. He paints word pictures of the deep lush green temple precincts and also of villages and people devastated by the war.[1] Those Olive Hitchcock refers to as the God-bearers in this jaggedly torn situation, those working for just reconciliation for all, and there are many in Sri Lanka, including many in the churches of all denominations and in the other faiths on the island, have perhaps suffered most when all they have striven for has on occasion blown up in their faces.

Harry Haas was a Roman Catholic priest and founder of the Woodlands Network in Bandarawela. He died in September 2002. I have visited the centre, high up in the hill country. It is the hub of a network of groups who work for the care and appreciation of the land through organic farming and appropriate, sensitive tourism. The groups also work for the

---

1. *Anil's Ghost*, Michael Ondatje, Bloomsbury, 2000.

development of the people, through the opportunity for literacy, practical skills and work. Harry spoke recently about the horror which overtook them all in the community of the small upland town when an open rehabilitation camp for young Tamil Tigers, which had enjoyed good relations with the local people, was suddenly, due to the voicing of extreme opinion on both sides, rejected by the same local people. The outcome was horrendous when 1000 villagers stormed the camp and killed all 40 of the young people, while the police stood by. Two of the boys killed were local Tamils from the tea estate, who had never been Tigers.

Chandrika Kumaratunga comes from an old and leading Sri Lankan family. Her mother was the first woman prime minister in the world and she herself is now the President of Sri Lanka. She has said quite recently,

> *We must with humility examine our failures . . . We must proceed with fortitude to face the daunting challenges of terrorism and the political and social violence it has engendered within the entire social fabric of the country.*

President and people are striving to keep the fragile peace of 2002. The new government was elected at the end of 2001 and a new Prime Minister, Ranil Wickramasinghe, was elected with a commitment to work for peace. The leader of the Tamil Tigers, Velupillai Prabhakaran, has committed himself to the peace process. People of all the faiths of the island have organised prayers for peace. The National Christian Council, under Ebenezer Joseph of the Methodist Church, is very active in relief work, in dialogue and in conflict resolution as is the Roman Catholic Church.[1]

The present situation in Sri Lanka was not evident when the Sinhala and Tamil people first went there, most probably around 500 BCE. According to the tradition the Aryan Prince

---

1. *Praying for Peace*, Andrew Wingate, *Church Times*, 20 September, 2002.

Vijaya came from the area of Bengal in north eastern India to found the Sinhala community, whilst the Dravidian Tamils came from South India at the same time. The tradition is that Prince Vijaya married a Dravidian from Madurai in South India and that his followers also married Dravidian women from Madurai. The Sinhala people developed the Buddhist religion in Sri Lanka, and today Buddhists are 69 per cent of the population in the country, which has a total population of over 18 million people. The Tamil people took the Hindu religion with them to Sri Lanka, and today Hindus are 15 per cent of the population.[1] Both the Sinhala and the Tamil people have contributed to the building of the country. In the past there was a lot of cross fertilisation between the people and their religions. The Moors and Malays went to Sri Lanka much later as traders and have made a good contribution. The last permanent group of people to arrive were the Tamils from South India who went there in the nineteenth century to work as labourers on the tea plantations.

There were three main colonizations of Sri Lanka. The Portuguese settled in the sixteenth century and stayed until the seventeenth century, taking their Christianity, Roman Catholicism, with them. Roman Catholics are still the largest group of Christians in the country. All Christians make up just under 8 per cent of the people, but their influence is far greater than this statistic would imply. One reason for this is that Christianity cuts across the ethnic groupings, so Christians have the opportunity to provide the link between the peoples, and some, especially in recent years, have done this very well indeed.

The Dutch colonized Sri Lanka from the seventeenth century until the end of the eighteenth century, taking their Reformed Church with them, and they were followed by the British, who stayed until the country gained independence in

---

1. *Out of the Depths. Struggle and Hope in Sri Lanka*, Christians Aware, 1992.

1948. The British took the Anglican Church to Sri Lanka and also Methodism.

Over the centuries the Church of all denominations in Sri Lanka has had many great achievements including the development of education, health and the social services. In recent years the Church, and the many church related organisations which have grown up in response to the collapse of the economy and the ethnic unrest which has led to the violence, are involved in inter-faith dialogue, work for those who are poor and work for justice and peace for all. Solidarity and sharing are at the top of their agendas.

All the colonial powers changed the economy of Sri Lanka from a simple peasant economy to a plantation economy, with plantations for tea, rubber and coconut. There were peasant rebellions in the nineteenth century, but the twentieth century saw the development of the plantations and the need to import some of the food to feed the people. By the 1950s Sri Lanka had developed into a welfare state with good administration, road and rail services and education and health care. The literacy rate was high and the death rate low.

The beginnings of today's crisis began in the 1960s when the prices of the plantation crops were falling and the prices of the imports were rising, so that by the end of the decade Sri Lanka was almost bankrupt, and tempted into the fashion of the time, borrowing money. The 1970s saw the development of the open market economy, the arrival of the multi-national companies and great material advances in a few areas, accompanied by unemployment and poverty in many areas.

With the development of the crisis situation in the economy there was a growth of unrest and in 1971 there was an uprising in the South of Sri Lanka, led by the Janatha Vimukti Peramuna, the JVP, which the government controlled by seeking help from overseas. More than 5000 people were killed, mostly young people and mostly Sinhala, and many more were arrested.

Alongside the unrest which grew from unemployment and poverty, since the independence of the country in 1948 there has been a growing dissatisfaction amongst the Tamil people, who have felt increasingly marginalised. For example, in 1956 Sinhala became the official language of the country and many Tamils, who could speak neither Sinahala nor English, could not communicate. An incident in Jaffna in 1974 has left a sad memory and has surely influenced the course of events since then. In 1974 there was an international convention of Tamil scholars during which a crowd gathered and became unruly. The police fired and killed nine Tamil people. The Tamils demanded a separate state in 1976. This was refused and the ethnic divisions and clashes have grown from there to the present day. There was communal violence in 1977 and in 1983. I visited Sri Lanka in 1984 for the first time and saw for myself the destruction of buildings and the sadness and fear of the people. At the offices of the Centre for Society and Religion in Colombo, whose director until recently was Father Tissa Balasuriya, a Roman Catholic priest and Oblate Father, I met people from every community who had lost their homes and members of their families in the violence.

There was a peace accord and the arrival of the Indian Peace Keeping Force in 1987, but after a lull the violence returned. The JVP revived in the south of the country and since then there has been sporadic violence and counter-violence accompanied by marches, demonstrations and strikes. The JVP was crushed in 1991. The governments over the years have generally responded to the troubles by repression and militarisation accompanied by a complete breakdown of confidence. President Kumaratunga has tried to begin a new phase, but the violence has continued, until the latest, 2002 commitment to peace, which has not yet stood the test of time.

Those who have suffered most from the troubles in Sri Lanka are, as they are everywhere in the world when trouble arises, the ordinary people. One Christians Aware visitor, in 2000, wrote about her concern for the ordinary people she met.

> *The people who live with this constant tension have my respect and admiration, their spirit, though knocked and attacked, has not been broken, they are proud people, a people who desire peace in their land and desire it now.*[1]

Another visitor in February 2000 spoke about his visit to many villages including Manampitya, a village 12 kilometres east of Polonnaruwa, a famous pilgrim place.[2] The people in this village are living a very hard life. The police take villagers in for questioning regularly and keep them for a long time. This means that they can't work and the families have become impoverished. The people try to take their cattle to the forests for the day and when they succeed the police often stop them bringing them back in the evening, so there is no milk. One man in the village spoke of losing his property in 1992, when 17 houses were burnt down. He is unable to get any compensation. Another village was visited where seven women have lost their husbands because they have been abducted and killed. Many women everywhere have lost their sons. Until recently people have been abducted from their fields and from their boats. The land of one person was taken by the chief monk of the nearby Buddhist temple, who told the Tamil people to go away and then gave the land to Sinhala people. The monk has now been assassinated. In a land where religion is so often a force for good, it is also, as it may be anywhere in the world, sometimes used for very bad purposes.

In Welikanda, a village 18 kilometres east of Manampitya, 26 Sinhala villagers were killed by the Tamil Tigers in 1995,

---

1. Carol Gotham, writing in the Spring 2001 *Christians Aware* magazine.
2. From the account of Tony Comber, Archdeacon Emeritus, Diocese of Ripon.

which resulted in many people leaving the village to go into Sinhala or Tamil refugee camps. The refugee camps are large and the people in them desolate. Often they have to live on emergency rations which are not adequate. Sometimes the people are living in open halls and sometimes in small wooden houses. In one incident near to Welikanda the army was clearing an area when two village people shouted 'Tigers' and they were promptly killed by the soldiers. Later 23 soldiers were killed. In a nearby village there have been 15 attacks by the Tigers in the last seven years.

The north of Sri Lanka is suffering particularly. The Tamil people are poor, the roads are in a terrible state and it is not easy to move anything, even essential items.

In most of the country most people are trying to carry on, especially now there is the 'promise' of peace. The little girl who lost her brother and then wrote a poem is not untypical. She wrote:

With determination we can conquer problems
in this lovely world,
though parents have lost children,
but there is no place for affection and love; violence rules.
What shall we ourselves do? We must think.

Now, with the new promise of peace, people are returning to their villages in hope. But, they are not yet returning to their farming because they are still afraid to be exposed in the fields. This means the people are dreadfully poor and sometimes they sleep in the forests because they are afraid that their homes may be attacked under cover of darkness. Often families are too afraid to allow their children to go to school so they arrange home teaching.

The economy of the country continues to be at a low ebb. The main industry should now be tourism, but it is almost non-existent and the hotels are almost empty. If the peace holds the government has plans to boost tourism.

The remarkable and hopeful sign is that there are organisations and people who have always risen above the troubles to share and be in solidarity with those who are oppressed. They are shining examples of courage and of hope for the country and they have a special opportunity, which they are making the most of, now that long term peace may be possible.

The people known as the 'Tea Tamils' must be among those who have been most oppressed in the country. It is perhaps because they arrived in Sri Lanka from South India in the nineteenth century to work on the tea plantations, when most other people were very well settled, that they have lived in something of a vacuum, alone in their simple communities, working long hours for very poor pay. Paul Casperz is a Jesuit priest who risked his life when he began to work in solidarity with the tea workers, sharing their lives, when he realised just how poor they were. He founded the multi-faith organisation 'Satyodaya', which campaigns for a rise in the price of tea on the international markets and also constantly challenges the government to improve the lives of the tea workers.

Annathaie Abayasekera was honoured by the Diocese of Kurunegala when it celebrated its 50th anniversary, for her work with women, on social issues and for peace and justice at national and international levels. Her main work in Sri Lanka has been with the tea plantation workers, and especially with the women, many of whom work long hours and are malnourished. She started this work in 1974 and has remembered all the opposition she faced as she met and talked to the women and then began work to raise the women to the level of the men on the plantations, and at the same time to get the women to develop their own self-worth. She has also, through her organisation, 'Penn Wimochana Gnanodayam', worked for education, organisation and training for the women. Much of her work has been done through mime, street drama and song. The programmes have enabled the women to challenge those who oppress them, and to grow as leaders, but their conditions of work have not improved very much yet. They still work longer hours and are more poorly paid than the men. Annathaie appreciates her friendship with the tea workers. She has written, 'I have learnt through interaction much more than I learnt through my university education. These women have minimal book learning but the depth of wisdom they offer is amazing and life sustaining'.[1]

No one has done more to build understanding and sharing between the ethnic and religious groups than the Roman Catholic priest Tissa Balasuriya, mainly through his thinking and work at the Centre for Society and Religion in Colombo. His theology is one which pushes him to strive for wholeness, in individuals, local communities, nations and the whole world. It is rooted in his belief that all that exists is created by God, who loves and cares for it. I will always be grateful to Tissa for my introduction to Sri Lanka when he took my group first to a simple fishing community at Negombo and then to his home in Colombo where we washed at the well. This was fun for us, away from home and with time to draw the cool and refreshing water, but it also led us to think of those who have to wash not only themselves but their children and clothes at the well throughout their lives.

Tissa sees the need for a new world order, where all people, of both sexes and of all races, creeds, nationalities and ages are respected and are thereby empowered to contribute. His work on behalf of women included his book, *Mary and Human Liberation*, when he wrote that Mary, mother of Jesus, was an ordinary woman, and could therefore be the inspiration for ordinary women everywhere. This book caused the Vatican to excommunicate him, though the excommunication was later rescinded. Tissa feels that lack of respect for other people implies lack of respect for God, and that the beginning of respect is to approach other people in

---

1. From *Love your Neighbour as Yourself*, Annathaie Abayasekera, *Christians Aware* magazine, Autumn 2000.

the humble way of learning, particularly when the approach is about religion. He writes, 'God does not leave any people without the means necessary for their spiritual growth and fulfillment'. He has brought people opposed to each other in the ethnic conflict together for talks and he has worked with people of other faiths at the Centre for Society and Religion for many years. He has made a special contribution to the Christian understanding of Buddhism.[1]

The Buddhists of Sri Lanka have their hard core of extremist opinion, which is difficult to win over because it is tied to vested interests. All the religions of the island have their intolerant and extremist elements of course. The position of the Buddhist monks and nuns is crucial for the future of the country. Some of them have made a great contribution towards peace work, as members of inter-faith groups and through the opportunities they always have to offer temple hospitality. There is a fine tradition of spiritual leadership in such people as Venerable Dharampala and Venerable Mahinda Thera. There are Buddhist leaders now who are working for reconciliation and peace, such as Venerable Punnyasara Thero of Gokarella, the leader of the successful movement to restore the ordination of bhikkunis or nuns in 1998, after a lapse of seven centuries. He is a patron of the World Solidarity Forum.

On 23 September 2000 the tenth anniversary of the World Solidarity Forum for Justice and Peace in Sri Lanka was celebrated at its central office by the lighting of the lamps on the tree of reconciliation. The tree, circling the globe, was created by Chandana Kumarasiri of Palugasdamana, Polonnaruwa. It symbolises the growth of the movement for peace and justice throughout the world. The lower circle of lamps represents the many grass-roots branches and

---

1. Books by Tissa Balasuriya include: *The Eucharist and Human Liberation*, Orbis Books and SCM, 1977; *Planetary Theology*, Orbis Books, 1984; *Mary and Human Liberation*, Cassells.

groups of the forum in Sri Lanka and the upper circle of lamps represents the branches and groups throughout the world.

The World Solidarity Forum for Justice and Peace in Sri Lanka was founded in Thailand in May 1990 with 90 representatives from 19 countries. Sri Lanka provided the leadership and sent 23 representatives to the launch. The membership of the forum in Sri Lanka is from the four religions of the country, Buddhism, Hinduism, Christianity and Islam, and also from the three main ethnic communities. Membership is taken from all over the island. The peace workers receive special training.

One of the founders of the forum, who is also one of its most active members and its Co-Coordinator is an Anglican priest, Yohan Devananda, who founded the centre of Devasarana near to Kurunegala in the 1950s. Devasarana has been important for Christian and Buddhist dialogue, reflection and action. It has been part of the movement for peasant organisation and, since the escalation of the war situation, for justice and peace. The experience gained in the evolution of Devasarana was taken forward into the World Solidarity Forum.

The Sri Lankan group of the forum has organised a fairly continuous programme of study, dialogue and action. It has also arranged, often in collaboration with other peace and justice groups, public demonstrations, peace walks, house to house visiting, exchange programmes, street dramas, publications, campaigning and lobbying. The Christians Aware representative to the tenth anniversary celebrations came home enthused by the street dramas which aimed to involve young people in peace work by vividly expressing the horrors of war. Some of the visits of the forum have been to refugee camps and to the north of the country, to stand in solidarity with those who have suffered most from the war torn situation. There is an important focus on action and dialogue at the grass-roots level, based on the firm belief that the basis of all peace work is the building of trust between the people.

Members of the forum have suggested that a 'Truth Commission' similar to the one which did so much good work in South Africa, could now be set up in Sri Lanka. They challenge people on all sides not to try to change the 'others' but rather to change themselves into the best they can be from their own religious and cultural standpoint. Great efforts are also made by the forum to pressurise the religious and secular power centres. The statement of *Samadana Pradakshinawa* or 'sharing of peace in the streets,' was signed by a long list of people of faith in Sri Lanka and Britain in March 2002, and is a challenge to 'taking to the streets in a movement for peace on the basis of justice for all sections of the people. From city to city, village to village, house to house. There will be discussion, house to house visiting, personal encounter, public meeting and public procession. People of all religions, communities and parties, people as well as leaders, will join together in a common effort . . .'[1]

It is a tribute to the work of the World Solidarity Forum that the challenge of *Samadana Pradakshinawa* is being taken up by people of faith, and particularly in the churches. This should not be surprising because 'samadana' is a deeply religious concept meaning 'sharing of peace.' 'Dana' means giving, but it is also the principal of sharing, which is at the heart of all religions, bringing about equality in society and leading to peace.

Duleep de Chickera is the recently appointed Anglican Bishop of Colombo who has worked for reconciliation throughout his ministry and is involved, with many others of all Christian denominations and other faiths, in the 'sharing of peace in the streets'.

Duleep told the story of how he went with two women and another man to Madukande, a suburb of Vavuniya, a town on the edge of the troubled northern region, to share in a programme for reconciliation between Sinhala and Tamil

---

1. From *Samadana Pradakshinawa*, World Solidarity Forum, March 2002.

villagers, in 1995.[1] Those involved in the programme sat on mats and shared informally. They included representatives of the local Sinhala and Tamil communities and a Buddhist youth group. Ananda Hamaduru, a Buddhist, introduced the gathering and suggested that the communities could consider building a pre-school together. Then he digressed from his prepared speech and told everyone present a family secret, that his brother had married a Tamil who had now become a close and loving sister to him. He told of how he had accompanied her and her baby on a bus journey from Colombo to Vavuniya, when people had stared at them, not being able to appreciate that they were friendly, never mind brother and sister, members of the same family.

Duleep responded to this story by telling his own story of being the child of a mixed marriage, with a Buddhist branch and a Christian branch to his family tree. And then the stories continued, until it became clear that there were others who also came from mixed families. The village chieftain was able to say with enthusiasm and support that everyone was part of the human race, so 'racial prejudice' must end. The chieftain went on to say that the foolishness of the prejudice which was suffocating the country was easily seen in the story of the times of tension in Vavuniya, when members of the community would leave their homes and spend the night in a ditch only to wake up the next morning to find people from the 'other' community also hiding in the same ditch. The chieftain ended his speech by calling on the whole community to join forces to clear the land for the pre-school and to build a road linking the two villages. Tea and food were then served and people talked in small groups. Duleep wrote afterwards, 'Listening to other voices, we were drawn to consider a deeper encounter with Christ the reconciler'.

This is a wonderful example and encouragement for

---

1. The story is told in *Nifcon News*, Lent 1996 (Nifcon is 'Network for Inter-Faith Concerns', a network of the Anglican Consultative Council).

Christians who are working with their sisters and brothers of other faiths to bring long life and strength to the new and fragile peace of Sri Lanka.

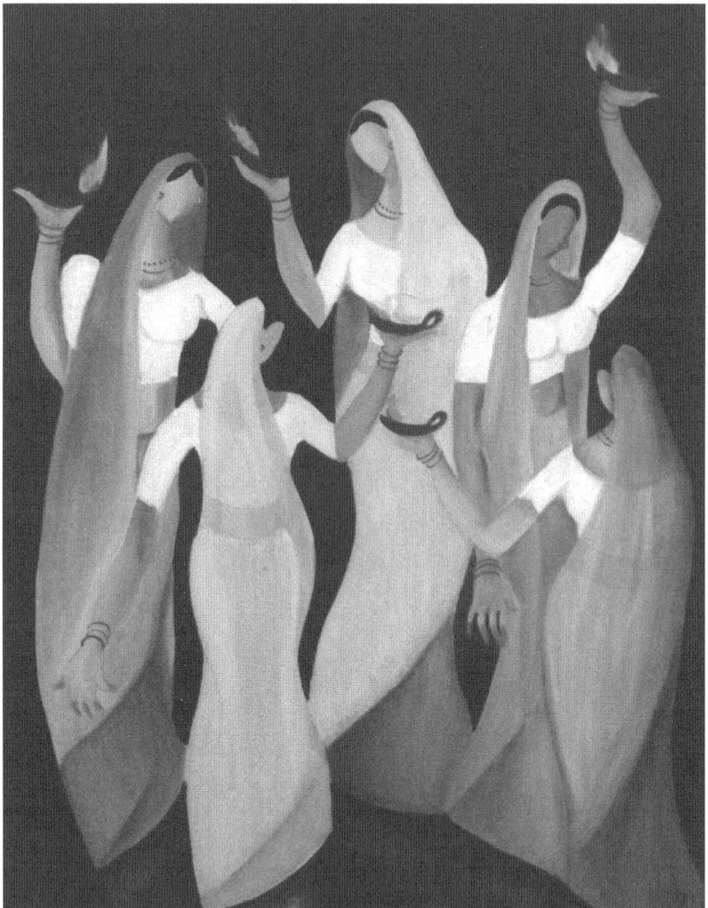

Women at Work in South India

For I was an hungered and ye gave me meat: I was thirsty and ye gave me drink: I was a stranger and ye took me in: naked and ye clothed me; I was sick and ye visited me; I was in prison and ye came unto me.
St Matthew 25:35-36

It's dawn
and shafts of light
set ablaze fields and thatched roofs
like a burst of conscience
revealing men and women,
girls and boys,
young and old,
choked by oppressive systems,
chained to endless poverty,
walking barefooted
to sweat on other men's lands,
or toil as coolies in the scorching sun
for seasonal wages;
that often wend their way
to liquor shops or gambling dens,
and empty stomachs
cry for better health care and education,
housing and light,
employment and basic needs,
for themselves,
for their children,
and dream of a better future
reaching out
to a sky full of stars.[1]

---

1. Poem by Savithri Devanesen, Director, Roofs for the Roofless.

Mrs Savithri Devanesen, whose love and compassion for the poor people of India shines through her poem, is someone who has dedicated her life to work in the villages of South India. I met her when I took a group to stay in Chennai and to learn about her endeavours in many villages near to the city. She began her involvement almost by accident when she gave some of her jewels to a poor family, so that they could put a roof onto their house. She and her husband discussed what she had done, and decided it was not enough and could never be effective, except for the family she had helped. She asked herself what she could do for all the other poor people who lived in the villages and the answer was very simple, and yet also very difficult, it was to organise with the people for change over a large area.

She began to make plans and in 1981 she discussed possibilities with the people in just one village, Vengaivasi. She soon included a whole cluster of villages and the charity 'Roofs for the Roofless' was born.[1] The obvious and first need of the people in the early years of the work was for rain-proof and reliable houses. The traditional houses were of mud and thatch and they soon crumbled. A brick-making kiln was set up and eight houses and toilets were built by the people themselves. This early success attracted the state government to approach 'Roofs' to ask for help with simple housing for the people. By 1985, 21 houses for landless families had been built in the village of Panaiyur. By 1988, 75 houses had been built for landless families in other villages, and by 1991 a further 100 houses had been built. Since then the building of simple and sturdy homes has gone on, from strength to strength. Savithri Devanesen, who is a member of the Church of South India, when reflecting on her work, has said that the houses of the people were like the mustard seed which galvanised her and the village people into action. Out of those small beginnings a huge variety of other work has developed.

---

1. 'Roofs for the Roofless' Flat 5, College Park Apartment, 4A, Manonmaniammai Street, Kilpauk, Chennai, 600 010, India.

Savithri Devanesen realised very early in her work that it was vitally important for her and her staff to talk to the village women. Change is never accepted and put into practice by the people in any country or culture unless it is accepted and practised by the women. Women, who do most of the work in the home, hold the key to their families' health and general welfare. Members of 'Roofs' talk to the women regularly and they articulate their problems and share their ideas for a better future for themselves and their families. The women in the early discussions asked for training in farming and gardening, and they were given seeds. Some women were given loans and training to start the rearing of poultry. Some began to keep goats and others learnt to make baskets. Some have formed cooperatives. A new centre has been built at Karanai which particularly benefits the women in offering them a place of meeting and community. It is also a centre where many of the training classes are held.

Schools have been started in most villages, and the children come to them after their day's work is done, to learn to read and write and to listen to stories and play games. The young people are offered skills training and are helped to discuss the issues that affect them. A programme of education for the women has also been developed. They learn to read and write. They learn health care and nutrition, and also to organise life and work. The possibility of family planning is introduced. Health clinics are now established in the villages, with health workers and visiting doctors. Leprosy camps are held and TB patients sent away for treatment. I remember the doctor in the eye clinic, who I saw working with a huge crowd of very poor and seemingly very old people, most of whom were in their forties and fifties.

A huge problem which the women in many Indian villages face is the alcoholism of many of the men. One way forward in dealing with this problem, which has been worked out by the women working with 'Roofs,' is for the women to unite together to speak out to all the men, so that one man in a family does not feel attacked, perhaps responding with violence. The women speak in the public meetings about how alcoholics ruin their families, throwing them into debt and therefore not only destroying their own health but also the health of their wives and children.

Water has always been in short supply in the villages, and efforts have been made by 'Roofs' to enable the people to dig many wells, so that all the people can reach them. They have also managed to persuade the state government to sink some bore wells. The relationship with the state government has been a special success for 'Roofs.' A particular benefit has been the encouragement the charity has given to the government to build good roads from the villages to the city, so that produce and craft work may now be sold.

The poorest of the village people always suffered because their animals were badly fed and were vulnerable to every possible disease. One new initiative by 'Roofs' has been the establishment of the veterinary care programme, with trained assistants and centres, and a fully qualified veterinary surgeon. The centres offer emergency assistance at any time, and also vaccination programmes and artificial insemination, to up-grade the stock and the supply of milk. More and more animals are treated each year, and the quality of animals in the region has improved out of all recognition. A fight was fought with those with vested interests, and some common land was retrieved on which to grow fodder for the animals. Poultry and rabbits have also been introduced to the villages.

One project which stands out for me in my visits to the many projects and people in the huge area covered by the work of 'Roofs for the Roofless' is the weaving project. Weavers have been helped to free themselves from the grip of 'master weavers' and to form cooperatives. The weavers now have good homes and good, solid work sheds. Many of the weavers in the cooperative live together in a village which caters for their needs, including a store and an office which help with the sale of the beautiful cotton and silk cloth they produce. I remember the beauty of the cloth, plain and durable cottons and stunning and brightly shining silks. I remember the pride with which the weavers worked. They are no longer among the millions of the downtrodden who live below the poverty line in this vast country. However, at the beginning of the twenty-first century, it is estimated that almost 36 per cent of the people of India, 329 million, mostly in the villages, live below the poverty line.

India is the seventh largest country in the world, covering 1.2 million square miles. It has a population of over 1 billion, and is the largest democracy in the world. It is divided into three natural regions: the Himalaya mountain region, the Ganges plain region and the Deccan plateau in the centre and the south. India includes many ethnic groups and languages. Life expectancy for the people of India has doubled since the country gained its independence in 1947, and is 62 for men and 61 for women.[1]

It is said that there are 1652 mother tongues in the country. Hindi is spoken by 66 per cent of the population and English by only 19 per cent. The issue of English is always contentious, because it is not only the language of the judiciary but also of higher education. Some people would argue that as many children as possible should learn English in the primary schools, so that those who are suitable can proceed to higher education. Others say that the majority of the children, who attend non-fee-paying schools, should learn their mother tongue and Hindi.

Seventy-nine per cent of the people are of Aryan origin, and have developed the Hindu faith and community. The Hindus are 79 per cent, Muslims are 13 per cent, Christians are about 2.4 per cent, Sikhs are 2 per cent, and Buddhists are 0.8 per cent of the population of India.

The constitution of India was designed between independence in 1947 and 1949, to make sure that India was a

---

1. Statistics from the United Nations Population Division.

secular country, where no particular religion or group would dominate, but all would be allowed to flourish in the freedom which had been fought for. The Mahatma Gandhi worked especially for this vision. The first democratic elections took place in the winter of 1951 to 1952. They gave equality in voting to the scheduled castes, as the former outcasts were now known, and to women. Unfortunately discrimination against the poor and against Christians and Muslims, and even persecution in some areas, has escalated throughout the 1990s.

Some historians would say that Hindu nationalism was growing throughout the twentieth century and was clearly visible in the years immediately following Gandhi's assassination in January 1948. Recent Hindu nationalism has not sought to change women's traditional roles, but rather to focus on the mother figure as the goddess in the home. In the most ancient Hindu scriptures, the Vedas, the waters are called 'mothers,' or givers of life and of purity. Both a mother and a river are venerated in India.[1]

The work of Savithri Devanesen and of others like her has helped to change traditional attitudes to women in India, where they have in practice and until very recently been seen as secondary to men. Some people would say that they are still seen in this way by many people. Almost everything conspired against women in the recent past; the culture and traditions of the people and also the religions of the country, including Christianity. Hinduism, the religion of the majority of the people, is patrilineal and patriarchal. Women traditionally go to live in their husband's family where the hope is that they will give birth to sons.

'A little son is the light of the house',[2] the little six-year-old Durga was told by her neighbours when her baby brother was born in a story set in India and written in 1929. Many

---

1. *Waters of Fire*, Sister Vandana, Amity House, New York, 1988.
2. *Pather Panchali*, Bibhutibhushan Banerji, The Folio Society, London, 1971.

hundreds of Indian girls alive today are told the same thing. Jessie Azir, herself a Christian worker from the Tiruneveli Diocese, who is currently working in the UK, has written in 2002, 'There is no doubt that our society is a patriachal society'.[1]

The Dalits are those who are outside the caste system of Hinduism. They were traditionally known as the outcastes and then, in independent India, as the scheduled castes. Gandhi called them the children of God or 'Harijans'.

Arundhati Roy has written about the outcastes of Kerala:

They were not allowed to touch anything that Touchables touched, Caste Hindus and Caste Christians. Mammachi told Estha and Rahel that she could remember a time, in her girlhood, when Paravans were expected to crawl backwards with a broom, sweeping away their footprints so that Brahmins or Syrian Christians would not defile themselves ... When the British came to Malabar, a number of Paravans ... converted to Christianity and joined the Anglican Church to escape the scourge of Untouchability . . . It didn't take them long to realise that they had jumped from the frying pan into the fire. They were made to have separate churches ... After Independence they found they were not entitled to any Government benefits like job reservations or bank loans at low interest rates, because officially ... they were Christians, and therefore casteless. It was a little like having to sweep away your footprints without a broom. Or worse, not being allowed to leave footprints at all.[2]

There are perhaps 170 million Dalits in India, and they are in reality, regardless of constitutional law, prohibited from drawing water from the village wells, from entering the village

---

1. Jessie Azir, writing in the *International Anglican Family Network* on 'Women and the Family,' Spring 2002.
2. *The God of Small Things*, Arundhati Roy, Flamingo, 1997.

temples and from eating in restaurants.[1] They are expected to have a house of lower structure than the caste Hindus, and to emphasize their humility, their houses have a very low entrance. Even today in the Christian communities and churches the Dalits are sometimes pushed away into a separate group or corner of the building. The word 'Dalit' means oppressed, broken people. The Dalit men, especially in the rural areas, often perform the most menial tasks and are completely marginalized. Dalit women are oppressed by everybody, sometimes including their own husbands, who are often so frustrated and badly treated that they explode in violence when they go 'home'. It is said that every day three Dalit women are raped in India, and it is said that sometimes this is done by non-Dalits as a punishment to the Dalit people.

Women in rural India, and also in the urban slums, may never have been to school and will, even today, be channelled by their families into doing all the household work, including carrying water, washing clothes and cooking. Many women and girls also work as domestic servants, in factories and on the roads. Rural women and poor urban women are often in very poor health. Sometimes the little girls are fed less than the boys, and women less than men. Women also have a tendency to sacrifice themselves, and to give any available food to their children. I remember seeing a notice in a slum community centre on 'How to increase your weight'.

The laws of India since independence in 1947 do give women legal equality, but attitudes and customs take longer to change than laws. Government, non-government organisations and the churches have introduced many programmes to give women a better chance to contribute to society. Savithri Devanesen realised early in her work that the education of the village women was the key to development and this has now been recognised much more widely, so that formal and in-

---

1. *Caste Out. The Liberation Struggle of the Dalits in India*, David Haslam, Churches Together in Britain and Ireland, 1999.

formal educational programmes have been introduced in many places, though in 1995 only 38 per cent of women were literate in India, as opposed to 52 per cent of men.[1] Recent work by the World Bank has shown that in some rural areas only 10 per cent of the women can read and write. In areas where Christian missions have been strong, however, many women and girls are literate. Kerala is an example of a state where girls as well as boys have good education. The literacy rate for women in Kerala is as high as 90 per cent. Christian schools have aimed to educate ordinary people, including the girls, for more than 200 years, and the churches in India continue this fine tradition today. Recently, towards the end of the twentieth century, women have also been given more opportunities to be economically self-reliant and to have more confidence.

The Young Women's Christian Association began in India, in Bombay, in 1887. It offered a community for women, and prayer, mutual help, and some training. It also offered safe places for women to live in the towns and continues to be important for today's women. Another important organisation which is working for women's development in India is the All India Council for Christian Women, which is the women's desk at the National Christian Council of India. This has offered links between international work for women through the World Council of Churches and the local churches throughout the country. This body has given encouragement and confidence to the local churches and workers, so that much more is being done by many of them today in every aspect of the development of women. Women's development is naturally leading to more general development and the raising of standards of health, well-being and confidence for previously deprived people, as mothers work to help their families and communities, though they help themselves last of all.

---

1. Statistics from United Nations Population Division.

The Roman Catholic denomination is the largest Christian denomination in India, but not the oldest, beginning its work after the arrival of Vasco da Gama in 1497 and clashing at first with the Christians who were already established along the Malabar Coast. The people known as the 'Thomas' Christians are the Syrian Orthodox, whose origins most probably go back to 52 CE. They are the ancient Christians of South India who had strong links with Persia and Edessa. Disputes with the Western Church led to a rejection of the Council of Ephesus by Eastern Christians and after 431 CE Eastern Christians were known as 'The Church of the East' with Syriac as the liturgical language. Some persecution of Christians in Persia and the rise of Islam in the seventh century CE resulted in the Church of the East becoming fairly isolated in South India. What developed there was a culture which was mainly aristocratic, Hindu in culture, Christian in faith and Syriac or Nestorian in doctrine, ecclesiology and ritual. Today there are several communities which claim descent from St Thomas.[1]

The Church of South India is the second largest church in India today. The Church of South India and the Church of North India are post-denominational churches as they were formed by the union of many churches. They are full members of the Anglican Communion. The Church of North India was formed in 1970 and has 24 dioceses. It has a special link with the Church of South India and the Mar Thoma Church (a reformed Syrian Orthodox Church) through a Joint Council which was formed in 1978 and which recognises similar work and aims.

The Church of South India, CSI, was formed in 1947 and has 21 dioceses. It was formed from the Anglican, Methodist, Congregational, Presbyterian and Reformed Churches. The dioceses all have a bishop and synod. The synods elect a moderator or presiding bishop for the Church of South India

---

1. *The Indian Christians of St Thomas. An Account of the Ancient Syrian Church of Malabar*, Leslie W. Brown, Cambridge, 1956.

every two years. The first synod was held in Madurai in March 1948 when Arthur Michael Hollis was elected as the first Moderator.[1] The original vision of the Church was that there would be spiritual as well as physical unity, but this did not happen easily, and many would say that it has never happened. Each diocese still knows which Christian tradition it comes from and parish culture and worship can be very formal and isolating. Some people from the CSI say that the great early vision of the church is being fulfilled, but not through what are seen as the important structures and hierachy of the church. The spirituality of the CSI can be seen more clearly at the grass-roots level, in brave lives, lived out in working for peace, kindness and understanding to someone 'other' within local community. The path to an Indian spirituality which is real and which is making a difference may be found where ordinary people toil, where the children are born, go to school and grow, where the families live and eat, and where people meet each other naturally.

A wonderful community opportunity began in South India when Victor Premsager introduced what is known as VELCOM into the CSI. Velcom is the 'Vision for Equipping Local Congregations in Mission.' The hope of the vision is to develop the church at the local level as a caring, sharing and serving community. Vital to this mission is the challenge to the local church congregations to be the missioners, including everyone in the community in their work, of all religions and of all conditions. It includes the rich and the poor, the educated and the uneducated, the high and the low castes and the Dalits. Naturally, because this is a community based initiative, women play a key role.

The CSI has stipulated that women should be given a 25 per cent membership on all bodies at every level of church

---

1. The story of the early CSI is told in *Led by the Spirit. A biography of Bishop Arthur Michael Hollis*, Constance Millington, Asian Trading Corporation, 1996.

life. It has been possible for the dioceses to ordain women since 1979, though they have not all done so yet. There is an Association for Theologically Trained Women, which offers theological education for women. The Union Theological Seminary in Bangalore, which I have visited, has a Department of Women's Studies. Members of the department are committed to women's development and to challenging those in the CSI who resist women's ordination and leadership. There are practical projects which women students get involved in. For example, some of the students have links with destitute women and their children.

Vishranthi, the mother house of the CSI order of sisters, is in Bangalore. It serves as a retreat and meeting house for the CSI as well as being the mother house of the community. There were 27 sisters and ten probationers when the order was inaugurated in 1952. The order has grown steadily and most of the sisters live and work in the villages of South India. The only qualification which is necessary to become a sister is a sense of vocation together with a dedicated willingness to serve. The community is bound together in prayer and the keeping of the rule of life.

The Church of South India Women's Fellowship has branches in many places, including the most isolated and inaccessible villages. It has started many programmes of awareness raising and general education. It has 210 preschools in rural areas where there were no schools of any kind and where children of all backgrounds and castes come together to play and learn. This is wonderful work and it has so far helped 6000 children. Women are also involved in sinking wells and planting trees in many areas. Hundreds of trees have been planted in North Kerala for example. In Coimbatore every family has been given a coconut sapling and the reports are that they are cared for lovingly.

The Diocese of South Kerala, through the Women's Fellowship and the local parishes, has focused on ministry for and by women for several years. In practice this has meant getting to know a cross section of women in the diocese, including the many who suffer the terrible evils of their society: alcoholism, drug addiction, homelessness and abuse including battering. The Women's Fellowship has been transformed from just being a time of fellowship and prayer and the giving of charity to being a movement for planning and working for change in society. Planning and action include how to boycott and destroy arrack shops, where people get drunk on the highly alcoholic drink made from sugar cane. Campaigns include how to fight against the government plans to dump garbage in the villages, and how to encourage women to be candidates for election in the local Panchayats or councils. Counsellors have been trained and counselling sessions are offered to suffering women. Many of them have grown in confidence, sharing their stories, working for change in their lives and also helping others. One congregation collected together some girls who were unskilled and unemployed and taught them how to make clothes and sell them for a small profit. Another congregation is teaching girls to do embroidery and to make bags.

One of the main problems the women have, as Savithri Devanesen discovered also in the villages near Chennai, is the alcoholism of their husbands. In the Women's Fellowship in Kerala the women are helped to encourage their husbands to join anti-addiction units and to accept medication and counselling.

The story of Susheela is the story of a woman who had to face a drunken husband every night of her married life. Not only would her husband be drunk but he would also demand good meals to eat, even though he had himself spent all the money on his addiction. If there was no food he would fly into a rage and smash the pots and pans and beat Susheela up. He would then bang out of the house and go to eat in a village shop, often borrowing the money, and leaving Susheela and her two daughters frightened and hungry. Susheela had to feed her children and therefore took work building roads or houses, or sometimes helping in another home. She could cope with her hard life early in her marriage, but then she became weaker. When the Kerala Diocesan Women's Fellowship met Susheela she was very frail, but she had one accomplishment which they immediately used for her benefit. When she was a young girl she had learnt to do embroidery, and the fellowship engaged her as an embroidery instructress. She now earns a regular income, her husband is improving through counselling and she is able to help other battered women. The local embroidery industry is flourishing.[1]

The women in Kerala learn the Magnificat and as its meaning comes home to them they become more confident and capable. Magnificat is a song of revolt against injustice and against those who are proud and haughty. It is a promise of good things for the poor and downtrodden, for all slaves and labourers, and especially for women who are oppressed.

> *God straightens up women who are bent down by evils in society like gender discrimination, dowry and exploitation ...*[2]

Jessie Azir has written about the work her own diocese does with women.[3] Jessie's home is in Tiruneveli, which was established by the Society for the Propagation of the Gospel and the Church Missionary Society 250 years ago. The first convert to Christianity in this diocese was Clarinda, a Brahmin woman who had a great gift for building bridges between the castes, classes and religions in South India. Women's education and health care are quite well developed in Tiruneveli,

---

1. Susheela's story is included in *Greater Peace, Closer Fellowship, Fuller Life*. Edited by Lily and Sam Amirtham, published by CSI Golden Jubilee Publication, 1997, p. 268.
2. *A Kerala Magnificat*, Lily and Sam Amirtham, p. 267 in *Greater Peace, Closer Fellowship, Fuller Life*, 1997.
3. *International Anglican Family Network*, Spring 2002.

because of a long line of excellent Christian women, which continues today in the many theologically trained women, though none of them are ordained yet. Jessie herself was the secretary of the Diocesan Women's Fellowship for six years and Director of the Counselling Ministry in the Diocese for five years. Jessie firmly believes that women have more capacity to care for others than men. She talks about the many programmes run by women in Tiruneveli, including feeding programmes for the beggars and homeless people and the establishment of small-scale industries and businesses for women. The Women's Fellowship is trying to follow the example of Clarinda, and to break down the barriers between the many and disparate groups, castes, classes and religions. There is also an important project in the dry and remote north of the diocese.

Women are trained, some of them at the Christian Counselling Centre in Vellore, where people go to be trained from all over India. The Christian hospital at Vellore is an inspiration for women. It began a hundred years ago from the vision of one woman, Dr Ida Scudder. The trained women visit the isolated villages, teaching in the pre-schools and running adult literacy programmes. They are strengthened for their work by reading the Bible and by meditation and prayer.

The women of India, of all the religions, are, and always have been, those on whom their families, communities and country depend. They uphold the faith and traditions of their people while some of them are managing to challenge those features of faith and tradition which are crushing to some sections of the communities, including themselves. They work inside and outside their homes, in menial and in highly professional roles. They are often exhausted, often oppressed, but those who stay alive are never finally defeated.

A story told by the late Mother Teresa of Calcutta is typical. She was called to go to a Hindu family with eight children who were hungry. She took some rice and gave it to the mother of the children. The woman took the rice and divided it in two. She took half the rice and went out into the darkness. When she returned Mother Teresa asked her, 'Where did you go?' The woman said, 'They were hungry too'. They were her neighbours, a hungry Muslim family.

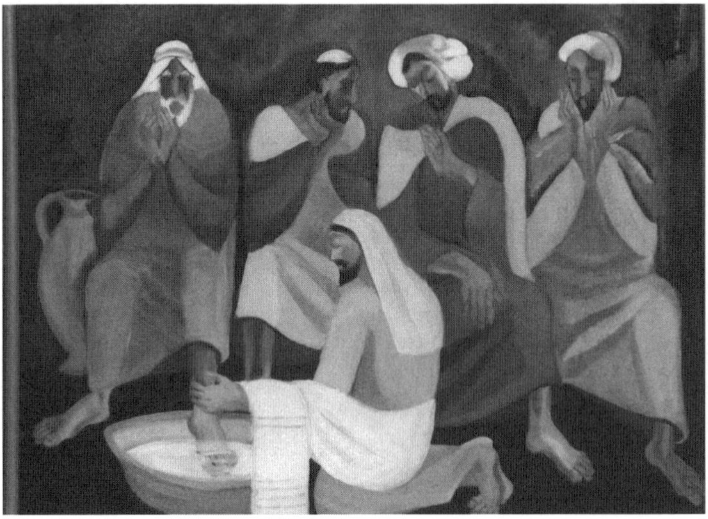

Suffering and Service in Pakistan

He riseth from supper, and laid aside his garments; and took a towel and girded himself. After that he poureth water into a basin and began to wash the disciples' feet, and to wipe them with the towel wherewith he was girded.

St John 13:4-5

A memory which will always stay with me is of attending a conference in Canterbury in the Spring of 2002 when we, the participants, were asked to sit down one evening to watch a video. We were asked to watch the video in a very matter of fact way so that I, and many others also, were not prepared for the content. The film, made in October 2001, showed the mourning, preparations for burial and burials of sixteen people of all ages, including children, who had been massacred while they were worshipping in a church in Bahawalpur, a town in Pakistan. It was harrowing to watch the video but what it must have been like to be one of the people in the church who saw the killings and survived, I can never know.

There are many suffering Christians, as well as many suffering people of other faiths, around the world, in many countries, and all in terribly sad situations. It is in recognition of this reality in our world that a Christian forum has been formed in Britain to support persecuted religious minorities around the world.[1] The forum aims to enable the sharing of information, to raise awareness of the plight of many suffering people, to encourage prayer and action, and to respond appropriately as a forum. 'Our determination to realise this vision is an obligation and commitment to our faith.'[2]

---

1. The Christian Forum in Support of Persecuted Religious Minorities Worldwide is supported by a range of mission and human rights groups. Partnership House, 157, Waterloo Road, London. SE1.
2. Bishop Mano Rumalshah, original visionary for the forum.

It is also vital of course that people of faith in countries where there is free speech encourage their governments to challenge governments where people are not so free. It is also vital to become more aware and challenging of the work of the United Nations. When Bishop Mano Rumalshah spoke before the Committee on Foreign Relations of the United States Senate in June 1998, the 50th anniversary of the United Nations Declaration of Human Rights, he supported the Nickels Bill, then being discussed, which offered a flexible response to suffering, including economic sanctions and the need for government to consult with non-governmental organisations, including churches, about human rights abuses and religious persecution around the world. He challenged the American Government and people to awareness and vigilance. He said,

> *Since the pilgrims first set sail in search of a place to practise their religious beliefs, religious freedom has been a cornerstone of your country's history and culture . . . You need to hear the cry of people around the world who suffer for their faith, who are denied the basic rights to believe, which you so naturally take for granted.*[1]

I have decided to write here about the Christians who suffer in Pakistan, but their story will inevitably point to many other places and people who need to be noticed, prayed for and worked with. At the launch of the Christian Forum for Persecuted Religious Minorities in June 2002 presentations were made on the suffering of Christians in Nigeria and on the suffering of Christians and Muslims in some areas of India. There are many other people around the world who suffer for many reasons, including their faith. For example,

---

1. Bishop Mano Rumalshah was Bishop of Peshawar and is now the General Secretary of the United Society for the Propagation of the Gospel.

many of the Southern Sudanese people are living in refugee camps outside their country because they are persecuted. Many of the people of Burma have fled to refugee camps in Thailand.

Pakistan means the 'land of the pure'. It was religion, Islam, which bound most of the people together when the country was founded in 1947. It was the first country in modern times to be formed on the basis of religion, followed in 1948 by Israel. Today 97 per cent of the people are Muslim, and the vast majority are Sunni Muslim.[1]

Pakistan is more than a country; it is also an idea, a cultural expression of identity. It is architecture, language, dress and food. It is a link in the chain that takes Muslims back to the past.[2]

Muslims had felt the need to organise as a separate group from the nineteenth century and right through the twentieth century. The All India Muslim League was founded in Dhaka in 1906 and the British Government recognized it in 1909. In the 1930s Mohammed Ali Jinnah became the Muslim leader and moved from working for unity with the other communities to working for the separate Muslim state which became Pakistan.

The partition which separated Pakistan from India in 1947 was far from peaceful. It is estimated that more than 2 million people were killed and 15 million people moved from their homes; Hindus to go to India and Muslims to go to Pakistan. An old friend, who is now dead, was the head of a college in the Punjab at the time of the Partition. He could never forget the slaughter of the people, including many of his own students. He worked for refugees throughout his life because of his experiences.

---

1. United Nations Population Division.
2. From, *Islam Today. A short introduction to the Muslim World*, Akbar S. Ahmed, I.B. Taurus, 2001, p. 127.

Jinnah called the new country 'moth-eaten' because it was in two halves. He began to wear the Muslim dress which is now the national dress of Pakistan and he fiercely championed Muslim dignity and the Muslim cause. However, he also said:

> *I am going to constitute myself the Protector-General of the Hindu minority in Pakistan.*[1]

and, famously:

> *You are free, you are free to go to your temples. You are free to go to your mosques or to any other places of worship in this State of Pakistan. You may belong to any religion, caste or creed – that has nothing to do with the business of the state...*[2]

His words may bring comfort and also give strength to the minorities, including the Christians, today as a vision for a future as well as for a very new Pakistan. The words never in fact became the reality, perhaps because Jinnah died in September 1948 and after his death Pakistan was so troubled that martial law was introduced in 1958, backed by the USA. Elections were not held until 1970, when Eastern Pakistan voted in the Awami League under Sheikh Mujibur Rahman, and Western Pakistan voted in the landowner, Zulfiquar Ali Bhutto. When Sheikh Rahman was arrested a government in exile was established in Calcutta, and the events leading to the creation of Bangladesh had begun. When up to 11 million refugees moved from East Pakistan into West Bengal in Indira Gandhi's India, the Indian army invaded East Pakistan and war broke out. India's soldiers marched on Dhaka and by December 1971 Pakistan had surrendered and Bangladesh was born. Many historians feel that this was the moment when Muslim power and confidence were crushed

---

1. *Islam Today. A Short Introduction to the Muslim World*, Akbar S. Ahmed, I.B.Taurus, 2001, p. 124.
2. From Jinnah's speeches, and quoted in *Liberty or Death*, Patrick French, HarperCollins, 1997, p. 363.

in the whole region and that this was one important reason for much of the Muslim aggression and intolerance which grew up in the newly truncated Pakistan. A glance at history in the region makes it clear that any hope that people of faith will live together in peace and harmony has to be worked for in every minute of every day.

Insecurity was perhaps the main legacy of the partition and the subsequent history of the country, especially at the time of the formation of Bangladesh, to the people of Pakistan. This was made worse perhaps by the weakness of the state when it was very new. It had a large army but also very little industry, large debts and the need to accept a huge loan from the Nawab of Hyderabad. The people, though mainly Muslim, were culturally varied; those who lived in what was Eastern Pakistan until December 1971 had felt very isolated. There was also the struggle between those who worked for Western style democracy, including President Bhutto and his daughter Benazir Bhutto, who was elected Prime Minister in1988, and those who worked for a military and strictly Islamic country. It is as members of a strictly Islamic country that the people of Pakistan have entered the twenty-first century. They have also entered the new era as members of a country which had become the first Muslim nuclear power in 1998 and which had developed a strong educational system and economy.

The people who are now Christians have lived in the area of Pakistan for thousands of years; an area where the ancient Indus Valley civilisation flourished. It is estimated that 95 per cent of the Christians in Pakistan are the descendants of Hindus of the scheduled castes, the labourers who did, and still do, the most menial work. The other 5 per cent are the descendants of converts from Islam and the caste Hindu communities.[1] The Jesuits arrived in the region from Goa in

---

1. Statistics from *The Terrible Alternative, Christian Martyrdom in the Twentieth Century*, edited by Andrew Chandler, Cassell, 1998, p. 103.

1579 when they were invited by the Mughal Emperor Akbar, an unusual man in his own time, who was interested in learning about many religions. Akbar paid for the first church to be built in Lahore. There was some persecution after Akbar's death, and the Roman Catholic presence almost disappeared until 1842 when the British conquered Sind. Most people converted to Christianity during the last 200 years, and particularly between 1880 and 1930. Since the country became independent there have also been conversions to Christianity amongst the nomadic Hindu tribes on the Indian border in Sind and the Punjab.

The Protestant presence began in the nineteenth century and the Church Mission Society was the most consistent and widespread influence. Very few people converted to Christianity until the Chuhras, beginning with one poor old man, decided to convert and very soon there were hundreds of Chuhra members in all the Christian denominations. Most of them were Christian by 1935. Their descendants are still Christian, and still doing the dirty and dangerous work. They are also, at the beginning of the twenty-first century, likely to be illiterate. The church buildings and the community of the church are vitally important for confidence building and education for the people.

The Church of Pakistan is the largest denomination in Pakistan today. It was formed in 1970 by the coming together of the Anglican, Lutheran, Scottish Presbyterian and Methodist churches. The Roman Catholic Church and the Salvation Army remain separate and there are also some free evangelical churches.

Christians have been isolated and persecuted, by fanatical and perhaps insecure Muslims, mainly since the formation of the country. Most ordinary Muslims, in the country and around the world, have been as appalled as their Christian neighbours by the persecution. It is also important to recognise that there have been times when ordinary Muslims have been attacked and killed by fanatics. Most women of Pakistan, of all faiths, are vulnerable in a society where both the culture and the laws work against them. There are of course very obvious exceptions, including some of the educated and politically astute women who are able to rise above the norms of their society.

Quamar Zia, who became a famously brave woman of Pakistan, was born into a Muslim family in 1929. She was sent to a government school until her father was ill, and then, at 17 years old she was sent to a Christian school in Madras where she read the Bible and became aware of God's grace and of the living Jesus. After the partition in 1947 Quamar moved to live in Karachi in the new Pakistan with her family. She lived for seven years as a lone and secret Christian until her parents began to arrange her marriage, when she ran away to work in a Christian orphanage. It was at this time that she accepted the name Esther John. Her parents' continued efforts to marry her to a Muslim led her to travel far away to the Punjab, where she lived and worked in a nurses' home and was baptised. The Bishop of Karachi arranged for her to continue her education and in 1956 she entered a Bible training centre where she stayed for three years. She then went to live at a Presbyterian Mission at Chichawatni. She cycled around the villages sharing her faith with the people. It was here that she was killed, on 1 February 1960. Her skull was smashed in while she was asleep. The murderer was never found.[1] It was Esther's courage in faith, and her joy, love and gentleness which led to her being included in the list of ten twentieth-century martyrs whose statues fill the niches over the great West door of Westminster Abbey. She, like the other nine martyrs chosen, represents the many Christian martyrs in her part of the world. The statues were unveiled by the Archbishop of Canterbury in the presence of the Queen, the

---

1. Esther John's story is told by Patrick Sookhdeo in *The Terrible Alternative. Christian Martyrdom in the Twentieth Century*, edited by Andrew Chandler, Cassell, 1998.

Duke of Edinburgh and people from all over the world on 9 July 1998.

Islamisation, following the amendments to the 1973 constitution, and the enforcement of the Islamic Shariah laws in Pakistan, has perhaps done more than anything else to make Christians feel second class citizens. For example, in 1979 the word 'freely' in relation to the practice of faith was removed from the constitution. Further, Christians are not allowed to stand as candidates for parliament to represent Muslims. Christians vote on a national basis, for Christian representatives in the National Assembly. The danger of this system is that local MPs may have little sympathy with the Christians in their areas. The Blasphemy Law has been the most difficult law for Christians to live under, and it has been used more and more since 1986. Since 1991 the law stipulates that if anyone has insulted Islam or the holy prophet, directly or indirectly, they are liable to capital punishment. This law has been the means by which people have been arrested and imprisoned and even killed. Nasir Saeed visited many victims of the Blasphemy Laws in Pakistan, and wrote a report.[1] Several suffering victims of the law were visited and their stories written down in the report. One of the recommendations of the report is that the death sentence should be abolished for those who are convicted under the law.

Bishop John Joseph was Roman Catholic Bishop of Faisalabad before he shot himself in front of the Sahiwal Sessions Court, where a judge had sentenced Ayub Masih to death under the Blasphemy Law in April 1998. The bishop had made many efforts to save Ayub Masih, including sending messages to newspapers throughout the country. He said,

The Christians of Pakistan are being held in a death sentence blackmail by the Blasphemy Law, under which their small

---

1. *Faith Under Fire. A report of the second class citizenship and intimidation of Christians in Pakistan.* 2002.

businesses are being taken over, their property is being seized and the situation is such that their women are not safe... Therefore,... in the name of my oppressed Christian people, I am taking my life.[1]

Bishop John Joseph was born in Khushpur near Gojra in 1932. He joined the Roman Catholic Diocese of Faisalabad in 1980 and became bishop in 1984. He was a well known worker for human rights and the Chairman of the National Justice and Peace Commission of his church. He was a loved and respected pastor and a doctor of theology. He was always at the forefront of the cause of religious freedom and always defended downtrodden people. He regularly attended rallies and demonstrations supporting the rights of Christians. He also championed women, children and poor workers. He was truly the voice of the voiceless in Pakistan and his death shocked peace loving Christians and Muslims alike.

There are many stories of suffering and persecution. I have chosen to write about only a few, but they represent all those who suffer. In February 1997 a mob attacked and decimated a whole Christian community in the Shantinagar/Khanewal area. A small boy gave an account of his own experiences.

We dared not cry, we could not shout for help. We had to hold our breath as we huddled together under the bed, so some human vultures were seeking to devour us. They had already desecrated our beautiful church and had set alight our precious books and other meagre possessions. They wanted to kill each one of us.[2]

There have been four fatal attacks on Christians in Pakistan since the 11 September 2001 atrocities, provoked by the

---

1. *Christians Aware* magazine, Winter 1999.
2. *Christians Aware* magazine, Winter 1999.

Pakistani Government's support for America in tackling the terrorism which afflicted its people so suddenly. Two of the attacks took place in August 2002. Six people died and four people were wounded in the assault on Murree Christian School near Islamabad. This school caters for the children of Christian expatriate workers in Pakistan, and many are from America. Gunmen broke into the school grounds on motor bikes and fired indiscriminately into the playground. There were no children in the playground, because it was raining, and the people who were killed were school employees, including security guards, a cook and carpenter and a receptionist.

Five women died and 23 men and women were wounded when worshippers in a Christian hospital in Taxila were fired on. Reports describe two craters in the ground where the grenades had exploded. The first woman to be killed was a 24-year-old nurse who was married with two young children. Her death is a sad reminder of the tragedy of the violence for the country and for the world. We are told that 'A dozen women's shoes littered the ground, mingling with the torn red fabric of four umbrellas, all shredded by shrapnel'.[1]

There is no doubt that the attacks on Christians are carried out by Muslim fanatics, and that most of the Muslims in the country are as sorry, sad and ashamed about it as are the Christian people. The President of Pakistan, Pervez Musharraf, went out of his way to condemn the August 2002 killings. He said, 'The attacks specially directed at our Christian brothers and sisters are the most shameful examples of terrorism'.[2]

A Muslim academic who visited the USA in the aftermath of the 11 September atrocity, to be in solidarity with the American people, was invited to speak in churches and to share his faith, a faith which challenges people to engage in a 'jihad' or struggle with themselves to become better Muslims, working for peace with justice in the world.

---

1. David Blair, writing in the *Church Times*, 16 August 2002.
2. Quoted in the *Church Times*, 16 August 2002.

The report of a group visit to Pakistan made me realise that the Christians there have made the best of their situations by taking the Gospel challenge to live and serve in the world, and not just in the church, seriously. They have understood that God is the God of all people everywhere and that their role is to work with and care for all the people in their country. Their response to their own suffering is loving service to all the people, and not just to the Christians. They see this response as their opportunity to enable God's love. Because Jesus came to the earth and lived with the people, they also have to be there, with the people in Pakistan, and especially with those who have been forsaken by everyone else, whether it is comfortable or dangerous. There is no alternative. A Pakistani Christian who gave a talk at a Methodist conference in June 2002 said that his only aim in life was to love and serve all the people in his country. When the Murree School was attacked John Malik, the Bishop of Lahore said:

As far as Christians in Pakistan are concerned, we will do our best to serve the nation in education, healthcare and other areas of work.

Health care and education are offered to whole communities by the churches. Christians and Muslims meet each other in school, and also in the health clinics which are run by the churches. The churches have pioneered work with leprosy patients and have recently established seven centres for those suffering from drug addiction. The church hopes to offer opportunities for people to set up small businesses.

The Christian hospital in Taxila, where the people were murdered in August 2002, is run by the Presbyterian Church with a mainly Christian staff. It specializes in eye care and has accepted people of all faiths for treatment since it was opened in 1922. It is typical of the dedication of the staff of the hospital that when the people were murdered the Friday and Saturday were spent in burying the dead, but on Monday the hospital was open for normal service.

Christians in Pakistan have always played their part in the care of the many hundreds of refugees who have gone there from Afghanistan since the late 1970s. An influx of 1.2 million new refugees entered Pakistan from Afghanistan in October 2001, when the American attacks on the Taliban and Al-Quaeda began. Some of the refugee camps are almost permanent and the people in them run their own affairs and even build houses, work places, shops and schools. There is a hospital, named after Sandy Gall, for the many hundreds of disabled people who need artificial limbs and wheelchairs. An important aspect of the work with the refugees is the training given to the women, so that they can sew, knit and grow crops, and thus support and encourage their families. There is also an effort to train teachers in the Afghanistan educational system, so that they will be really useful when they go home.[1]

Service for everyone in Pakistan, and especially for those for whom no one else cares, is the great contribution of Christians, especially over the last 150 years. The service offered is very often in response to suffering. It is noble and a challenge to all people of faith who seek to walk a loving spiritual path through life.

One event, of 150 years ago, took place at Bannu Hospital, in the wild area on the border between Afghanistan and Pakistan. Dr Pennel went to serve the poor people of the region, but they ignored him, seeing him as an alien from a far away and colonial land. After a long time of waiting and rejection the doctor saw a dog with a broken leg, which he put into a splint. When the dog walked out of the clinic wearing his splint the people saw immediately that he had been helped by the doctor. This was the turning point for the doctor and for the people. They realised that if the doctor could help a dog, a creature of no importance, then surely he would be able to help them. An act of simple and loving service

---

1. Some of this work is done by Ockenden International.

by someone who had been rejected was an important key to the future for the work of the hospital and for Christians in Pakistan. And the catalyst for the breakthrough was of course the dog.

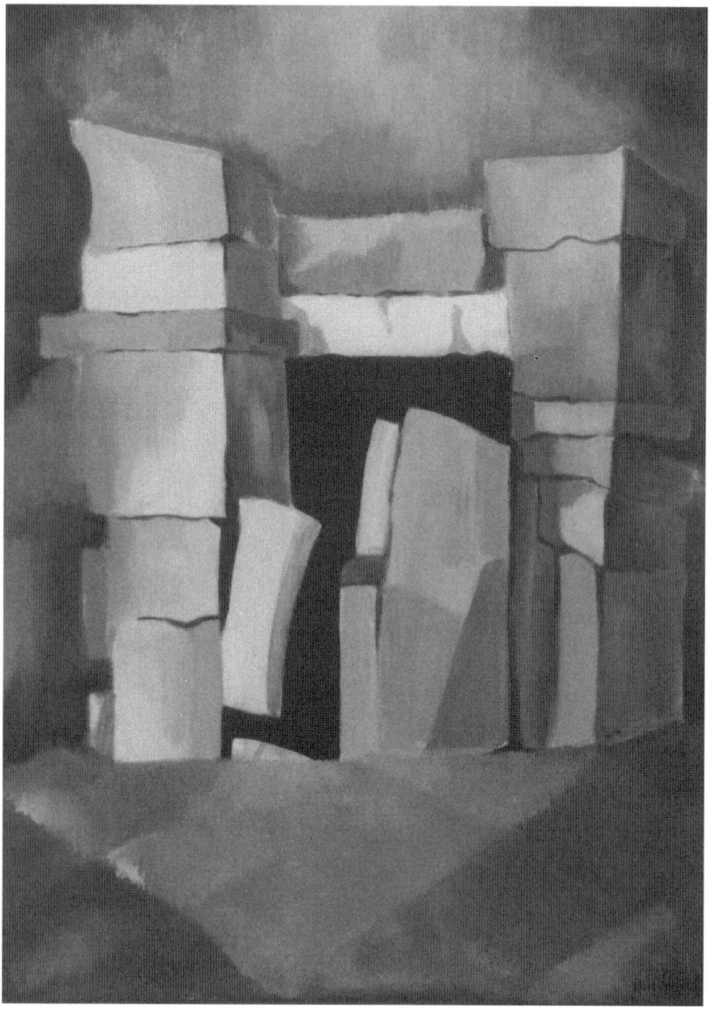

Healing and Hope in Bangladesh

Jesus said, 'Take ye away the stone' . . .
he cried with a loud voice, 'Lazarus come forth'.
And he that was dead came forth.
St John 11 1:39, 43-44

Now upon the first day of the week, very early in the morning, they came unto the sepulchre, bringing the spices which they had prepared, and certain others with them. And they found the stone rolled away from the sepulchre. And they entered in, and found not the body of the Lord Jesus. And it came to pass, as they were much perplexed thereabout, behold two men stood by them in shining garments: And as they were afraid, and bowed down their faces to the earth, they said unto them, 'Why seek ye the living among the dead? He is not here, but is risen . . .
St Luke 24:1-6

When John and Rita Bennett went to work in Bangladesh from the Methodist Church in the UK they spent their first summer of 1999 travelling and getting to know the countryside and the people. They have told stories of precarious travels, over frail bridges and along bumpy roads. They have travelled by steamer and rickshaw. They visited the national monument to those who died in the resistance movement which led to the country's independence in 1971. They found a place of peace and beauty, with gardens which are lovingly cared for.

Bangladesh has had many names in a long history which began when it was the ancient state of Banga. The British East India Company gave it the title of Bengal and it became East Bengal when India achieved independence in 1947. The partition of 1947 made it part of Pakistan, as a largely Muslim country. In 1956 it was known as East Pakistan and finally it became the independent country of Bangladesh in 1971. This was the time the people had been waiting for, the time when they were no longer over-shadowed and dominated by West Pakistan, but were able to express their distinct cultural identity.

John and Rita also went to a place which they felt was even more beautiful than the national monument, the Centre for the Rehabilitation of the Paralysed, coordinated by Valerie Taylor who is supported by skilled and dedicated Bangladeshi workers. They met doctors, therapists and the makers of wheelchairs. They met nurses and people who teach gardening and animal husbandry. They met the patients, including people who have suffered accidents at work, where there are few safety regulations. They met the children in the centre, most of them there because they were damaged in birth. Childbirth is a hard and risky experience for most women in Bangladesh, even today. Many of them do not have professional help. It is said that some of them eat as little as possible so that they will produce small babies and thus lessen the risks.

John and Rita met people who had been injured in their homes. This is not surprising in a country where keeping a home together is hard and sometimes dangerous work. Half the housing is of mud-brick construction and has no plumbing. One toilet may be shared by 50 families. It is estimated that more than 13 million people live in the shanty towns around the major cities.

One of the most serious and common injuries in Bangladesh is caused through the carrying of heavy loads, at home and sometimes at work. The loads are carried on the head and a sudden movement can cause damage to the spinal cord and thus to the central nervous system

The main hope of the work at the Centre for the Rehabilitation of the Paralysed is that the patients may one day return home, to live as normally as possible with new hope for an independent future.

An exciting development for the centre has been the making of a full length feature film called *Bihongo*. The film is based on the real life stories of the patients at the centre. It has been produced using famous TV actors who worked voluntarily or for very small fees. The story is an exciting one, including drama and romance, and including a wicked uncle and a car chase. The hope of the film is that it will change attitudes in a society where there is very little understanding of the disabled people, who are often seen as useless and irrelevant. The film has being dubbed in English so that it can be shown in the UK.

It is hard to change attitudes to disablement in a country where literacy rates are low and where girls especially leave school very early. Only 13 per cent of girls receive secondary education.[1] The schools are poor and poorly equipped, but there is hope in the dedication of the Church. Rita Bennett was invited by the Church of Bangladesh to train teachers to offer the best possible education to the children. The new government has committed itself to the cause of the children of the country. In April 2002 the President, Prime Minister and Leader of the Opposition all signed pledge forms to commit themselves to the cause of children as a priority.[2] Quality education needs to be the priority of course, so that teachers are trained in diverse methods and skills, and so that resources are readily available.

A good example of a small business which works to train young people and is dedicated to giving young people a good start in life is Drik Computers. The young people who go to Drik are trained as photo-journalists. They are also helped to plan their careers. This business is a secular organisation run by Muslims, which promotes minority rights, women's rights and human rights in general in Bangladesh. The members put on exhibitions of the photographers' work and of carpet manufacturers' work.

---

1. *The State of the World's Children*, 2002, UNICEF.
2. *The State of the World's Children*, 2002, UNICEF, p. 45.

The development of the country has not always been impressive, but rather troubled and turbulent. The constitution, providing for parliamentary democracy, was adopted in December 1972. An affirmation was made of democracy, secularism, socialism and nationalism. It was sad that the initial hopes were not fulfilled, partly due to economic fragility, and that by 1974 a state of national emergency had been declared. In January 1975 civil rights were suspended and the trade unions and opposition parties were banned, leaving the Bakshal, mainly made up of Awami League members and pro-Moscow communists. In August 1975, Sheikh Mujibur Rahman, the first President, was assassinated by a group of army officers and martial law was declared. General Zia ur Rahman founded the Bangladesh Nationalist Party and won the 1978 elections. In 1981 Zia was killed and an army coup under General Ershad was successful. General Ershad formed the Jatiya Party and won the 1986 election.

In 1991 Ershad was deposed and Bhegum Khaleda Zia was elected as prime minister. Five months later a parliamentary system of government replaced the presidential system. Women voted for the first time in the 1996 general elections and Khaleda Zia kept her position, but unrest and violence led to her fall and to the election of another woman, Sheikh Hasina as prime minister. Social unrest has continued.

Bangladesh is made up of a fertile alluvial plain where rice, tea and jute are grown. There are also rainforests and swamps. The climate is not easy to live in, with heavy summer rains and hurricanes and floods from June to September. There are very few mineral resources, only a little coal and natural gas. As a glance at the short history of the country has shown, it has been very unstable since its foundation, added to which it is one of the poorest and most heavily populated countries in the world. The population is more than 120 million people.[1] The country has suffered many floods and famines.

---

1. United Nations Population Division.

Much of the budget is taken up in paying debts to the rich nations. Forests are being destroyed by Bangladeshi entrepreneurs. Bangladesh is working to forge trading relationships within the region and particularly with China, the new superpower.

In April 1991 there was a terrible storm, when nearly 100,000 people were killed and millions of people were left homeless. One of the main problems is that the good, rich earth has been concentrated in the hands of a few people. The varieties of rice grown have been much reduced, following the 'green revolution', and farmers are now much more dependent on the use of fertilisers. More than half the people, who are very poor, work on the land. Added to this the marine life along the coast has been harmed by spillage from oil tankers and by the discharge of sewage and industrial waste.

Christians and Buddhists are small minorities in Bangladesh. Muslims are 83 per cent and Hindus 16 per cent of the population.[1] In 1989 Islam was declared the official religion, which has made a great difference to the minority peoples, but also to many Muslims. An example of oppression hit the world headlines in 1994 when the writer Taslima Nazrin wrote a book called *Shame* which condemned the oppression of Hindu minorities. She was imprisoned for asking for more respect by Islamic law for women's rights.

The largest churches are the Roman Catholic and Baptist Churches.

Mrs Manjo Baroi is the headmistress of the YWCA school in Dhaka, and a leading Baptist laywoman. She has served on the World Council of Churches working party on 'Christianity, Poverty and Wealth in the twenty-first century'. She is someone who works in the gap between the rich and the poor in Bangladesh. She promotes women's and children's rights. She does a lot of work in confidence raising, which is as vital

---

1. United Nations Population Division.

as education for most women. She also works along with others to rescue and rehabilitate women and children who have gone over the border into India to become sex workers.[1]

The Church of Bangladesh was born from the Anglican and Presbyterian Churches in 1971 when the nation emerged. There was only the one diocese, of Dhaka, until 1990, when the Diocese of Kushtia was created. Bishop Barnabas Dwijen Mondal of Dhaka, who retired in September 2002, has always been well aware of how marginal to national life the church is, and of how easy it would be for it to merely exist. It has not done that but has rather deliberately taken on the role of working with people who are poor and broken, to bring hope and healing.

Martin Heath is someone who visited Bangladesh many times and who also represented the Church of Bangladesh in Europe. He has said that he has found it very difficult to get people in Western Europe to appreciate the Church of Bangladesh.

> . . . it is not easy for many in the Churches in Europe to recognise that the materially impoverished Bangla disciple, with his hands outstretched, is not necessarily waiting to be given something, but is rather offering something instead, a pearl of great price.[2]

The church does its work with the poorest of the poor in the firm faith that it is living and working with those who are loved by God, those who are where God is. This faith was expressed movingly and vividly by the great Bengali poet, Rabindranath Tagore. In his *Gitanjali*, or song offering to God, he wrote:

Here is thy footstool and there rest thy feet where live the

---

1. *Guilty Without Trial. Women in the Sex Trade in Calcutta*, Carolyn Sleightholme and Indrani Sinha, Stree, 1996.
2. *Towards a wider world. Partnership and the Church of Bangladesh*, Martin Heath, p. 308 in *Anglicanism. A global communion*, Mowbray, 1998.

poorest, and lowliest and lost.

When I bow to thee, my obeisance cannot reach down to the depth where thy feet rest among the poorest, and lowliest and lost.

Pride can never approach to where thou walkest in the clothes of the humble among the poorest, and lowliest and lost.

My heart can never find its way to where thou keepest company with the companionless, among the poorest, the lowliest and the lost.[1]

Social development programmes are promoted by all denominations in Bangladesh and are competitors for funding from many sources which makes life difficult for those involved, and especially for the smaller projects.

The Social Development Programme of the Church employs a staff of over 700 and more than half are women. Sixty-five per cent of the staff are Christian but there are also Muslims and Hindus.[2] The work of the SODAP focuses on small scale community based programmes and includes community health, agriculture, credit schemes, primary education, vocational training, women's cooperatives, adult education, forestry and irrigation.

In February 2002 two Christians Aware visitors went to Bangladesh and one of the first projects they visited was the SODAP development programme in Mehapur. Income generation activities are encouraged and enabled by loans, mainly to women of all the faiths. Help is given with the management of the loans and with health and nutritional education. There is also a children's health clinic. Women are helped to plan and prepare nourishing meals for their children. One good meal is a rice stew called hotch potch. The visitors stayed in a home where all the food was home-grown and cooked. Tripty Biswas is a resourceful woman who is the sani-

---

1. *Gitanjali*, Tagore, Macmillan, 1913 and 1992.
2. *Towards a wider world. Partnership and the Church of Bangladesh*, Martin Heath, p. 309 in *Anglicanism. A global communion*, Mowbray, 1998.

tation manager for her region, arranging for slab toilets to be installed and used. John, Tripty's husband, is the manager of the loans scheme.

In the 1980s the Church of Bangladesh established a colony for landless people down in the south in Barisal region. A community of Christians, Hindus and Muslims were offered land on which to build their own houses and later they were offered farm land on which they could grow food crops. Saving schemes are encouraged and then loan schemes. A fish pond was dug, a school built and a church erected to be shared by the Church of Bangladesh, the Roman Catholic Church and the Baptists. Rita Bennett visited the colony, where she saw men with their own rickshaws and working as rickshaw wallahs in the nearby town. She met a man who carved furniture and sold it in the towns. She met women who kept chickens and who were sewing on machines. Some people were making cement rings for simple lavatories. Some women had tea stalls or shops. The money earned by the people with their small businesses is very little, but it does give them new hope and something to work for, and it has already given them good homes which are neat and cared for, with decorations and plants.

Rita joined a women's seminar and discussion group on primary health care when she visited the colony near Barisal. She listened to a talk on the use of re-hydration salts in cases of diarrhoea. She remembered that the women joined in the discussion with grace and confidence. The local priest told her that the project had given them a lot of new energy. This was especially true of the Muslim women who had led very sheltered lives. The people are moving from being healed of lethargy and shyness into new hope and energy for the future.

Brother Roger of Taizé, speaking from his own experience of working for reconciliation in war torn France in the early 1940s has said that the heart of suffering is at the heart of true contemplation. His sacrificial and holistic approach to life has developed into a community of some 90 brothers from more than 25 countries and from Protestant, Catholic and Orthodox churches. It is a place of inspiration for young people from many countries. Tens of thousands of young people go to Taizé, once just a group of farm buildings in Burgundy, every year. There are also the Europe-wide gatherings and the small communities serving in deprived areas all over the world. There is a community of Taizé brothers in Bangladesh, near to Mymensingh. The brothers run a centre for the disabled. They concentrate on restoring the dignity of people who have been rejected by their communities.

The restoring of dignity to people who are broken in many different ways is at the heart of the work for healing and hope which energises so many people to give and do so much in Bangladesh. It is at the heart of the gospel challenge to the enabling of many people to come out of their many tombs to new life and hope.

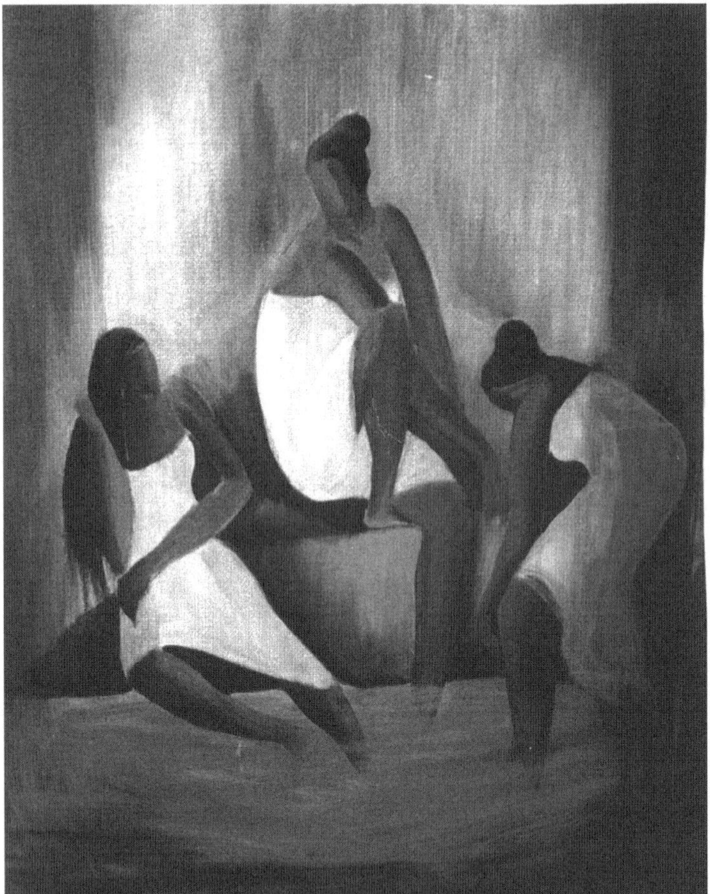

Community and Service in Japan

*He that is faithful in that which is least
is faithful also in much.*
St Luke 16:10

In the Autumn of 2001, as part of a visit to Hokkaido, the northernmost of the four large islands of Japan, I stayed in a family home on the shores of Lake Toya very near to the volcanic Mount Usu, the volcano which had erupted in March 2000. Every care was made to make me and my group feel at home, including the beautifully prepared rooms and the wonderful and complicated Japanese supper we shared with our hosts and Japanese friends.

One special experience we were offered during our stay was the opportunity to take a bath in the Japanese style, sitting in a deep pool of the water which bubbled from a natural spring and over granite rocks. Time had to be taken to enjoy and benefit from this 'exposure' and it did in a small way prepare us for the time when we had a bath in a public bath house, this time surrounded by strangers who were somehow a community.

My host and hostess near Lake Toya owned a rather unusual mountain near to their home. Shizowa Shawa is a mountain which grew up overnight in 1943 when a volcano erupted in one of their fields. We were invited to climb the mountain, wearing safety helmets, because the volcano is still active. Inspiration came to write a traditional Japanese poem or 'haiku' about this adventure:

*Steep forest path up,
to bare rock, warm underfoot.
Above, spouts of steam.*

As I enjoyed staying in a well cared for and loving home and visiting the surrounding area, including Shizowa Shawa and the volcano on Mount Usu, I longed to ask my hosts a question. I waited for a time, and then when we knew each other a little, I did ask why they had returned so quickly to an area from which they had recently been evacuated and which was still conceivably a dangerous place. The answer came very naturally as they explained that this place is their home and the people around them are their community, some of whom have not been as fortunate as they have, because they have lost their homes in the eruption and resultant floods and therefore need help. It would never have crossed my hosts' minds to stay away for longer in order to be safe.

Japan, in north eastern Asia, includes the four large islands of Honshu, Hokkaido, Shikoku and Kyushu. There are also 3000 small islands forming an arc between the North Pacific Ocean and the Sea of Japan, to the east of the Korean peninsula. The climate varies from tropical in the south to cool temperate in the north. There are very few natural resources and even the land available for cultivation is small, about 13 per cent of the total area.

The population of Japan is 126.5 million today, and about 78 per cent live in urban areas. Tokyo is the capital city, with a population of 34.5 million. Eight other cities have populations of over 1 million.

Nara was the first permanent capital of Japan, in the eighth century. This was later, in the ninth century, moved to Kyoto. Both Nara and Kyoto have been important places in the development of Buddhism. Gradually the warrior class or samurai emerged, followed by the power struggle between warlords and the emergence of the Kamakura shogunate in 1185, which was the first of a series of military regimes to hold power until 1868. The Kamakura shogunate faced Mongol invasions which were repelled. They were helped by a number of storms, which they called 'kamikaze' or 'divine winds.' Buddhism flourished during this period and several new sects emerged, including Pure Land Buddhism, which developed the focus on the community and on the saving power of the Amida Buddha.

The Kamakura shogunate was destroyed in the early fourteenth century and Emperor Go-Daigo re-established himself, though he was later expelled from Kyoto, and replaced by a puppet emperor by the military clans. Go-Daigo set up his court at Yoshino and for 56 years there were two imperial courts. The Onin War lasted 100 years and new military chiefs emerged who lived in fortified cities and developed trade with the outside world. It was at this time that Francis Xavier arrived and set up his mission. Towards the end of the sixteenth century the warlords became very isolationist and controlling. This led to Christianity being forbidden. In the seventeenth century the Tokugawa clan became supreme at Edo, which later became the city of Tokyo. They governed until 1867. They controlled the cities and compelled the chieftains to spend half their time on the shogun's affairs. A class system developed in which the samurai were the highest group, followed by peasants, artisans and traders. The policy of isolation continued, with the exception of the city of Nagasaki, where the Dutch and Chinese were allowed to trade. Isolation broke down in the nineteenth century, when the Americans forced the ports open, and the general chaos led to the resignation of the shogun in 1867, and the restoration of the imperial authority when the Meiji Emperor was established. This was the beginning of modernisation and of the Japan which is a world power today.

Modernisation resulted in the establishment of a constitutional monarchy in 1889, though the prime minister and his cabinet were responsible to the emperor who was seen as divine. (In 2002 Japan re-introduced this idea, which had been rejected at the end of World War II.) A Japanese army was created in the same period and replaced the power of the samurai. Japan won a war against China at the end of the nineteenth century and had control of Korea. Japan won the Russo-Japanese War of 1904-5 and annexed the Sajalin Peninsula. Korea was annexed in 1910. Japan was the ally of Britain in World War I and gained control over several German possessions in East Asia. Japan also extended its influence over Manchuria and Mongolia. The depression of the 1930s led the army to expand its power, while blaming and attacking the government for the situation. In 1931 the army occupied Manchuria without government permission, and then took over the complete power and the policy of aggression they maintained until their surrender, at the end of World War II, following the dropping of atomic bombs on Hiroshima and Nagasaki, in 1945.

US troops remained in Japan between 1945 and 1952. The country was forced to renounce the emperor's claim to divinity and to accept parliamentary government and an independent judiciary. In 1955 the Liberal Democratic Party was elected, and worked over many years, through alliances linked to the USA, for economic recovery and growth. There has been a movement away from farming, into the cities and into the production of goods dependent on engineering and high technology. The dominance of the corporations has grown throughout the late twentieth century, and in some ways their organisation is similar to the traditional system in that the employee is bound to the corporation as in an earlier age he might have been bound to his local warlord. Women are still not seen as part of this system, though more of them now work outside the home. Economic success is seen as most important, and even the family may be second to this. Towards the end of the 1990s the economy has suffered in the general crisis which has struck most of Asia, and there has been some unemployment and poverty.

Francis Xavier took Christianity to Japan in 1549. He set up a mission at Kagoshima. At first Christianity was tolerated, but in the late sixteenth century missionary activity was forbidden, and in 1637 Christianity itself was forbidden in Japan. Christians kept their faith secretly through all the years of persecution.

At Oiso, near Yokohama I have visited a museum which is full of examples of how the faith was practised in secret over more than two hundred years. There are crosses hidden in dishes, bowls, mirrors and wooden carvings. Some of the crosses are hidden in covered cavities in the backs of carved wooden Buddhas. There are also blocks of wood with relief carvings of Mary and Jesus. Sometimes these blocks of wood were used to print paper impressions which were used for testing the loyalty of Christians, who were asked to step onto them and who were killed if they refused.

When Japan was opened up to Western influence in the nineteenth century Christians were allowed to practise their faith in public again. A French Roman Catholic priest arrived in 1855. In 1859 two missionaries from the American Episcopal Church arrived, followed in 1860 by the first American Baptist missionary. In 1872 Ioann Kasatkin, known as Father Nikolai, established a branch of the Russian Orthodox Church in Tokyo. The Church Missionary Society sent the first English Anglican Missionaries in 1868 and more were sent by the Society for the Propagation of the Gospel in 1873. The first synod was held in Osaka in 1887 and this was when the Nippon Sei Ko Kai was officially established. Nippon Sei Ko Kai is translated as 'Holy Catholic Church of Japan' though the church is now known as the 'Anglican Communion in Japan'. The first Japanese bishops were consecrated in 1923.

Christians form a very tiny proportion of the population of Japan, something just less than 1 per cent, and are not therefore worthy of mention in the official statistics, which include Buddhists, who are 38.3 per cent of the population, and followers of Shintoism, who are 51.3 per cent of the population.[1] In practice many Japanese people are atheistic in their everyday lives, though a good proportion of them turn to one of the religions for special occasions. Babies are often taken to the Shinto shrine, marriages are often performed in

---

1. Statistics from United Nations figures.

a wedding chapel with a Christian ceremony, and the dead are often buried in a Buddhist ceremony.

I have visited the Anglican Church of Japan many times. Today there are 11 dioceses, all of them focused on service to the local community, the wider community and the world. Education is an important part of the work of service of the church, and its schools and universities are open to all, regardless of religion or lack of it. The schools are fee paying, but only for those who can afford the fees. I have visited many colourful and very happy and relaxed kindergartens and primary schools, where it would be remarkable if the children did not learn. The Church Missionary Society did a lot of the pioneering work to establish education, especially for girls. I have visited the Poole Women's College in Osaka Diocese, an excellent place of community and education which was founded by the CMS. Children are a privileged group in today's Japan, they are mostly bright and healthy, and are to be seen everywhere, with their families or on the many school outings which are arranged.

In 1995 I attended the opening of a new Christian university, the University of St Andrew, in the Osaka Diocese. The campus is very new and bright and impressive and the chapel dominates everything. The ceremony for the opening of the university was a Christian one, with a gathering of 1500 people, even though only 1 per cent of the students are Christian.

My 1995 visit to Japan was dominated by the aftermath of the 17 January 1995 great Hanshen earthquake, in which more than 6000 people died and 100,000 buildings were destroyed. I visited the huge earthquake zone which stretches from Osaka to Kobe and even beyond. I saw heaps of stones, collapsed buildings, buckled roofs and houses which, though standing, were lopsidedly dangerous. A cloud of dust hung in the air. I met people who lost everything in the earthquake, homes, friends and work places. I saw many potted plants, marking the places where people died. I also heard the stories of some of the people who had worked very hard to rescue those who were trapped, and who then continued to keep the community together. Yutaka Andrew Nakamura has written about the earthquake and about his efforts to rescue people from its destruction.

> *... a sensation similar to hammering was felt from below ... I was worried about the safety of Takeuchi-san, Suzuki-san and Furuya-san, who live near the church ... I headed for Suzuki-san's house. However the ordinary route was blocked by a huge house which had collapsed ... As I approached from the opposite direction, I saw Suzuki-san's neighbour's house completely collapsed and a few people ... rescuing the four people trapped in the house ... The atmosphere was absolutely terrible on the first night ... At 7.30 am the next morning I celebrated Eucharist for those who either died or are suffering from the earthquake ...*[1]

I visited Hokkaido in September 2001, and found that I was again invited to meet people who had suffered from a natural disaster, this time the eruption of the volcano on Mount Usu. However, the eruption did not dominate the lives of the people, even in the area where it took place. The matter of fact response was similar to the response of the people who suffered from the earthquake, that this was a natural occurrence and the important need was to help those who were affected and to continue life, without bitterness.

The visit, with a Christians Aware group, was to the Diocese and island of Hokkaido, the northernmost Japanese island. Hokkaido is spacious and beautiful, with rivers, mountains, forests, fields and modern cities. In summertime it is cooler than the rest of Japan, and in winter it is enveloped in enough thick snow to host a famous ice festival and winter sports activities.

---

1. *The Great Hanshen Earthquake – A Personal Account*, Revd Yutaka Andrew Nakamura, priest of St John's Church, Diocese of Kobe.

Farming and fishing have continued up to the early twenty-first century in Hokkaido, though there are currently issues of whether it is cheaper to import food than to grow it, and there is a fairly new problem of some unemployment.

Etsuko Maruyama has written about life in Hokkaido, where she now lives with her husband Keiji, having spent several years in England and then a short time in Tokyo.

People's lives in Hokkaido are not so easy. Winter is so severe and there are many mountains, including several active volcanoes like Usu. However, people live here with awe (probably more than the people feel in the Honshu area). While we were living in England, we were aware that we ourselves love to stay in natural areas rather than living in a city. This was one of the reasons for us moving to Hokkaido. Since we moved to Hokkaido we have felt that wonderful nature heals our bodies and spirits. This year, through visiting many places in Hokkaido with Christians Aware, and meeting many people, we felt that our wonderful nature sometimes turns into a very strict nature. Even in difficult days people live here quietly, and accept the difficulties. Nature is a gift from God. In any condition, in any time, God will guide us. We feel that people in Hokkaido believe in God's guidance keenly, through living in this wonderful and strict natural environment.

Hokkaido was only explored and settled by the Japanese people in the eighteenth and nineteenth centuries. Before that the indigenous people, the Ainu, farmed and fished. The Ainu people are something of a mystery. They are Caucasian but no one is sure where they originally came from, though it is possible that it was from the region immediately to the north of Japan. They went through a time of conflict in the nineteenth century, and then of absorption into the Japanese way of life through mixed marriages and the general decline in the Ainu culture.

The Ainu were converted to Christianity through a CMS mission under the leadership of John Batchelor, who arrived in Hokkaido in 1874 and walked to the area of Mount Usu to begin his mission. The mission was shared with his wife and their adopted Ainu daughter. John Batchelor and his wife later lived in Sapporo. Sadly few of the Ainu people kept their Christianity when he returned to the UK, where he died in 1944, though an Ainu priest was ordained in 1937. What happened to the Ainu raises interesting questions about the mission to them, which people say seems to have depended rather too much on the missionary who took it, and may never have been alive in the culture and hearts of the people.

Nathaniel Uematsu is the bishop of Hokkaido and his parishes are all over the island. In Hokkaido, as everywhere in Japan, the smallness of the Christian community is hard to believe because Christians are very active not only in the churches, but in the wider community and country. Nathaniel Uematsu was the General Secretary of the Province of Japan before he became bishop, and he was there when the May 1996 Synod issued a statement of regret for the part played by the Church in supporting the established role of the emperor and for the military aggression of the Japanese in World War II. Nathaniel has a special concern for reconciliation between the peoples of the world, and for respect and care for non-Japanese people living in Japan. There is a burnt cross in his diocesan chapel, which came from the wood of houses burnt in Bangladesh during the war there. It was placed in the chapel by visitors as a reminder of the challenge to all Christians to work for reconciliation and community through the cross, and as a symbol of the solidarity and support of the people for each other.

The Christian community is powerful partly at least because the commitment of the members is great, including spending every Sunday in church, sharing both worship and food, and planning. At St Margaret's Church in Sapporo on one Sunday in September, when I just happened to be there, a delicious lunch of lamb stew and rice was followed by discussion of plans for the bazaar and the sale of second hand clothes to the increasing number of very poor people on the island. At St Mark's in Asahikawa the community gathered to greet their guests and for an evening barbecue of rice, chestnuts, beef, salmon, miso, tofu and prawns.

'We can all do something,' could be the motto of the Christians of Japan, and it was put into practice very clearly in the area around Mount Usu, the mountain where the volcano erupted in March 2000, when the people of a huge area had to be evacuated. The story is an uplifting one in that, due to the swift and unauthorised action of a brave scientist, the evacuation of the area was ordered before the eruption and there were no deaths. The scientist took his reputation and his career into his hands when he took responsibility for ordering the evacuation without going through the normal channels of authority. The lives of all the people were saved but the devastation was tremendous and some of it will be obvious for a long time, in washed away roads, tons of black ash and destroyed houses. My visit to see the rim of the volcano, with the group and in the pouring rain, helped us all to absorb the spirit of the place.

One woman, Mrs Akiyama, spoke of her experiences, which were typical of many. When she knew she must leave her home she could already see falling stones and ran home to grab her cat. She then went to the high school in a neighbouring town, where 300 people slept in each room, and then on to an abandoned hotel. The cat had to sleep in the car. People came from all over a huge area to help the victims. When Sapporo city offered free houses for three months, Mrs Akiyama, her mother and the cat went to live there, though the cat had to be hidden. Now that she has returned home Mrs Akiyama, like my hostess in her beautiful home on the edge of Lake Toya, has spent a lot of her time helping those who have not yet been re-housed, some of whom are elderly and disabled. The atrocities committed in New York on 11 September 2001, when the World Trade Center was detroyed, were just a few days before I visited, and forced many victims of the volcano to re-live their own traumas.

The destruction of the World Trade Center has galvanised many Christians in Japan to work to raise awareness of the need for world community and peace. Sermons are being preached and talks are given. A lot of work has also been done by the churches since World War II to achieve reconciliation and friendship with churches and people in Britain.[1]

There is a growing respect and work amongst Christians in Japan today for human rights for the people who are not Japanese within Japan itself. These people include the Koreans and the Ainu. I was taken to the far north of Hokkaido, through the mountains and rice fields, to visit a memorial and Buddhist temple to Japanese and Korean people who suffered and died as forced labourers in World War II. There were photographs of some of the people who had suffered, and many colourful paper cranes, the traditional signs of hope in Asian culture. Many work camps for reconciliation have been held since 1945 and NSKK has a special concern for its service to the Korean people who remain in Japan and who are often poor and marginalised. The NSKK is also developing a link with the Church in Korea. It has further been pointed out by some Christians that the post-World War II development of the Japanese economy, including the expansion of trade and tourism, has also oppressed neighbouring countries and peoples.[2]

The NSKK has looked into its position in World War II, and into its attitudes to traditional Japanese society,

---

1. *The Witness of the Japanese Church to Reconciliation*, by Michael Ipgrave is included in *Open Hands*, edited by Barbara Butler and published by Kevin Mayhew, 1998. This chapter includes the work of the Japanese Church for reconciliation with Britain following World War II.
2. *The Nippon Sei Ko Kai Today and its Future Task*, Samuel Isamu Koshiishi, from *Anglicanism, a Global Communion*, edited by Andrew Wingate, Kevin Ward, Carrie Pemberton and Wilson Sitshebo, Mowbray, 1998.

including the role of the emperor. In May 1996 the Church made a statement of 'war responsibility' and issued an apology. The bishop of Tokyo spoke at the 50th anniversary of the dropping of the bomb on Hiroshima when he said:

> *When we travel to neighbouring countries of Asia, we hear many voices for the victims of Japanese atrocities during military invasions and occupations of those countries. For us to be committed to world peace, we have to overcome the misleading conception that it was only Japanese who suffered in war, as represented by the bombing of Japanese soil and our defeat.*[1]

The May 1996 Synod also examined and regretted its traditional prayers for the emperor and its support for him as reigning according to the will of God.

Although there was some acceptance, both before, during and after World War II, by the Anglican and other churches, of the military regime and its actions, it is important to be clear that this was not a uniform acceptance and that there were many Christians who opposed militarism and the war, and who were harassed, tortured and imprisoned. Many Anglicans refused to be registered as part of a war time Protestant grouping and they were also punished.

Raymond Renowden has written about his experiences in Japan at the end of World War II including his entry into Hiroshima after the bombing. He stayed in Japan for two years as an information officer and has told the story of his visit to Tokushima on Shikoku Island. The bombing of Tokushima had caused a blazing inferno during which many people died, and when Raymond Renowden got there the town was a wilderness of rubble and ashes. His story is about his meeting with Fujimoto Matsumara, a priest of NSKK

---

1. 'Message for Transfiguration Day 1995', John Makoto Takeda, from the NSKK newsletter, September 1995.

who was a graduate of Tokyo University and had studied at Ridley Hall, an Anglican theological college in Cambridge, in the UK. When World War II came Fujimoto was imprisoned and tortured by the Japanese Secret Police because they thought that because he was an Anglican he was a Western spy. He was not alone among Japanese Christians in being the subject of this suspicion. He lost his wife and two of his children in the war, but a son survived. He was released at the end of the war and went back to Tokushima to live, hungry and dressed in a loin cloth, in a shack in a shanty town. He held the services of worship for the people, and celebrated the Eucharist in his hut using rice and sake. People sometimes walked 12 miles to join the celebrations.

Raymond Renowden remembers that Fujimoto was not bitter about what had happened to him, but rather holy and very loving. Raymond has written:

He was truly alive, brimming over with faith, hope and love . . . His incredible courage and faith made a bridge for the future . . . Out of his apparent 'powerlessness' he continued to witness and minister to the small scattered remnants of the Christian community . . .

Fujimoto gradually developed the parish and rebuilt the church.

Throughout the visit to Hokkaido the CA visitors stayed with families and in church centres, sleeping in Japanese tatami rooms, in Japanese style. The Japanese rooms are cool and, however small, they feel spacious. They have special focal points, perhaps a painted door or a wall, a vase of flowers, or a picture. They serve as sitting rooms, dining rooms, bedrooms.

The Japanese room is like the Japanese Church, neat, beautiful and peaceful, but also ready for change and adaptable to many roles. This is a Church of focused love and readiness for active service.

THE MIDDLE EAST

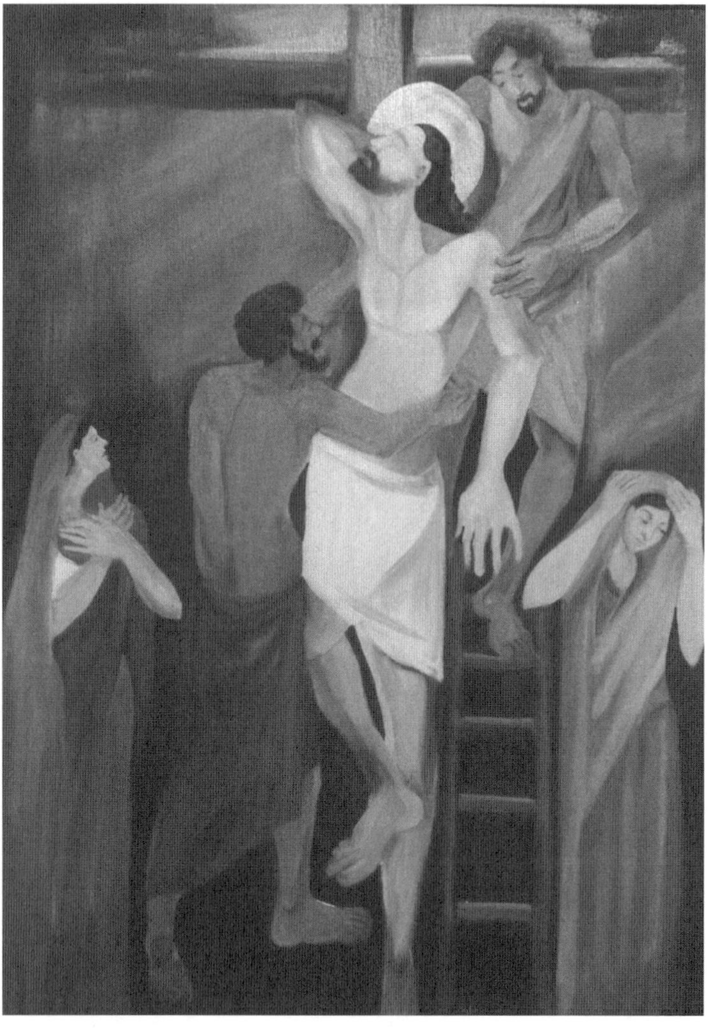

Cross Roads in the Middle East

And she brought forth her first born son and wrapped him in swaddling clothes, and laid him in a manger, because there was no room for them in the inn.
St Luke 2:7

And it was about the sixth hour and there was darkness over all the earth until the ninth hour. And the sun was darkened and the veil of the temple was rent in the midst.
St Luke 23:44-45

Mahmoud al Aloul was interviewed by a Western journalist in August 2002 as he sat in the home of a man who was shot dead on his roof in Nablus. The family had lost their father but were fortunate, at a time when 25 families were made homeless by house demolitions, to keep the roof over their heads. Meanwhile another Western journalist was visiting what is known as Israel's bus graveyard, the place where the buses are taken when they have been destroyed by suicide bombings during which many of their passengers have been killed.

The situation in the place Jews, Muslims and Christians call the Holy Land, the place where Jesus was born, lived and died is alarming, appalling, as awful as it was in the time of Jesus. When Jesus lived there Palestine was a place of grinding poverty for most people, with hard labour for the majority, cruel military occupiers and wealthy tax collectors. Crucifixion was a normal punishment for those who resisted the occupation. The Palestine of today is a world of growing unemployment, poverty, death and destruction but it is still the Holy Land. Dorothy Jean Weaver is a teacher at the Eastern Mennonite Seminary and lives in Bethlehem. She has written:

> *When God comes to be with God's people it is not to an idyllic, fairy-tale world . . . but rather to the real world of poverty, extortion, callous cruelty, unrelenting terror and inconsolable grief . . . This is our God, the one who comforts those who mourn, claims peacemakers as children of God . . . this is the good news of the Kingdom.*[1]

Bishop Riah Abu El Assal is the Anglican bishop of Jerusalem.[2] He has said that the 2002 occupation by Israeli forces of the Arab Evangelical home and school and the sending home of the children was symbolic of the depressing and dangerous emptiness of the Holy Land for many Christians. He has appealed to Christians all over the world to give love, encouragement and support to the Christians who live and suffer in the place where Jesus lived and not to remain at a distance, viewing the cross from afar. When Bishop Riah went on the 2002 Good Friday walk along the Via Dolorosa and joined the service in St George's Cathedral, he and everyone else felt that the sounds of helicopters, police sirens, gun fire and tank movements dominated everything. The atmosphere was very frightening, as it must have been 2000 years ago when Jesus was crucified. The streets were empty and people in all the faith communities were wondering what horrors would come next. Biet Jala and Biet Sahour have the biggest Christian populations of any of the Palestinian towns and they have suffered greatly. Kathy Pierson, an American Roman Catholic who has worked in a home for the disabled in Palestine has written of the time she spent in Bethlehem when the 'little town' was bombed together with Beit Jala and Beit Sahour. She has described the tanks entering the refugee camps and the havoc they caused but her main concern has been the traumatisation of the children and the subjugation of the people.

---

1. Dorothy Jean Weaver's article was included in the Winter 2001 *Christians Aware* magazine.
2. Bishop Riah has told his story in *Caught In between*, SPCK, 1999.

This homeland, this homeland,
deserves to be redeemed by our blood and hearts.
Shame on us if we slumber and lose a right
which we should preserve.
Rise up. Rise up.
Even if we suffer hardships
by our own hands we shall redeem
this homeland. This homeland.[1]

The ancient homeland of the Palestinian people, Palestine, was the area around Jerusalem which came under the British administration after the collapse of the Turkish Empire in 1917. It was bounded by the Mediterranean Sea, the River Jordan, Lebanon and the Sinai Desert. In 1917 most of the people were Arab, but between World War I and World War II a parallel Jewish community was built up. This was mainly due to British government policy at the end of World War I. The Balfour Declaration accepted the establishment of a Jewish homeland in Palestine, ignoring the presence of the Arab people who lived there. Balfour wrote to the British cabinet in 1919:

> *In Palestine we do not propose even to go through the form of consulting the wishes of the present inhabitants of the country . . . Zionism, be it right or wrong, good or bad, is rooted in age-long traditions, in present needs, in future hopes, of far profounder import than the desires and prejudices of the 700,000 Arabs who now inhabit that ancient land.*[2]

The Jewish community was further built up during and following the Holocaust and World War II. Jewish people poured into Palestine, seeking security and a home after the horrors

---

1. From *A Continent Called Palestine*, Najwa Farah, SPCK, 1996.
2. Balfour Declaration.

they had gone through in the concentration camps and the upheavals of post-war Europe. In a belated attempt to protect Arab interests, the British government resisted this emigration and, while the war was still raging, Jews were turned away from Palestine, some to be returned to Germany and certain death. This rejection of the Jewish people was part of a rejection of Jews which had gone on since the dawn of Christianity of course, for which many Christians all over the world have, in the twentieth and twenty-first centuries, begun to feel guilt.[1] This continual spurning of the Jews has made many of them determined that now that they have a homeland they will 'never again' lose it and risk being subject to the horrors of their very recent past. A former foreign minister of Israel, Abba Eban, who died in November 2002, said:

> *We have fulfilled our human vocation by redeeming hundreds and thousands of our kinsmen from sterility, humiliation and death . . . it is in Israel alone that the Jew can face the world in his own authentic image, and not as a footnote in the story of other societies . . .*[2]

A United Nations compromise proposed the establishment of two parallel states in 1947-8, one Jewish and one Arab but the hopes and dreams of Jews and Palestinians crumpled as open warfare erupted between Jews and Arabs before the plan could be implemented. Many Arabs had to flee from their villages and then Jewish settlers moved in. The now infamous massacre of 250 people of Der Yasseen, a village on the western edge of Jerusalem, caused fear to sweep through the Palestinian people, and many fled as refugees as city after city fell. Palestine was torn apart and divided between what became Israel and Jordan.

---

1. Many books have been written about the rejection of the Jews through the centuries.
2. Abba Eban.

It was at this point that the Palestinian people suffered terrible deprivation and marginalisation, which they have never recovered from. I attended a conference in England in 1993 called 'Christians in the Holy Land'. Palestinian Christians gathered from all over the world, to share a few days together and it was immediately obvious that no matter how well educated and comfortable some of them were, they were endlessly insecure, most of them living in exile, as they still are, and longing for their homeland. They sang songs of longing for home.[1]

Najwa Farah, a colleague of mine, is a writer and a Palestinian Christian. In her book, *A Continent called Palestine*, she said sadly of her family: 'Like all Arab Christian families, we could trace our origins back to the ancient church of the apostles.' She wrote of her trauma in 1947 when:

> *We were cut off from the world of the living and imprisoned in caves and camps, our condition deteriorating from one crisis to another . . . bewildered, shocked, broken-hearted, humiliated . . . I saw one city after another attacked and occupied, one village after another wiped out . . . my people becoming in one night refugees.*[2]

A Quaker woman, Jean Zaru, has written of her memories of 1948:

> *I can remember very clearly the fears, hiding in a basement, and the Palestinian refugees from the coastal plains of Palestine. My father and older brother, hearing their plight, took a truck with water and bread and rescued many of the children and women . . . About 50 of the refugees shared our house for about six weeks, another 100 camped under our pine trees.*

---

1. *Christians in the Holy Land*, Edited by William Taylor and Michael Prior, The World of Islam Festival Trust, 1994.
2. *A Continent Called Palestine*, Najwa Farah, SPCK, 1996.

An excellent book, which tells vividly of the displacement of the Palestinian people in 1948 is *Blood Brothers* by Elias Chakour. He is a Melkite priest and this is his story.[1]

In the 1967 war the West Bank was occupied by Israeli troops and taken from Jordan which later renounced interest in the area and put its weight behind the hopes of the Palestinian people for their own homeland. The West Bank soon saw the erection of many Jewish settlements and in a now familiar pattern, Palestinian villages were destroyed and olive groves bulldozed. Najwa said, 'It was like seeing a horror film twice'. Israel established a military rule in Gaza and took over East Jerusalem, so that the city was united but not free.

The issue of Jerusalem is perhaps the major stumbling block in the way of all negotiations for peace. It is said to be the most beautiful and most suffering place in the world. It is a city which is holy for the three faiths of the region, Christianity, Judaism and Islam.

Jews have always longed to be in Jerusalem. It is central to their worship and to their hopes. The Passover Festival marks the beginning of the Exodus and is a festival of exile, of longing and of the promise of the return. Participants were and are still reminded that the festival will be, 'Next year in Jerusalem'. Today when Jews go to Israel they go to pray at the Western wall, all that remains of Herod's great temple. They also go to Yad Vashem, the moving and magnificent memorial to the Jews who died in the Holocaust.

Jerusalem is one of Islam's three most holy places, with Mecca and Medina. Muslims have lived there and throughout the region since the time of the Prophet Mohammed in the seventh century. The al-Aqsa mosque is ancient and the Dome of the Rock is visited by Muslims from all over the world as the place from which the Prophet ascended into heaven.

---

1. *Blood Brothers*, Elias Chakour, Kingsway Publications, 1984.

Christians have lived in the old city since the first Pentecost and the building of the first churches there soon after the crucifixion and resurrection of Jesus Christ.[1] The indigenous church has survived now for over 2000 years, sadly only too often hidden from outsiders by a veneer of Western faith and culture linked to European imperial power. Most Christian denominations are represented in Jerusalem today, the Orthodox communities being particularly committed and obvious. The many churches and Christian communities in Jerusalem have not always been friendly towards each other. As a visitor to the Church of the Holy Sepulchre I, like most other visitors, was told stories of rivalries and quarrels about this and other pilgrim places. Recently progress has been made by the churches in working together, perhaps forced by the political situation, but also encouraged by the sterling work of the Middle East Council of Churches.

Christian pilgrims have gone to the Holy Land from all over the Christian world from the very early centuries after the crucifixion and resurrection, especially at times of festivals. It is possible that there are fewer pilgrims now in the early twenty-first century than ever before in the history of Christianity. The troubles have meant that the pilgrim places are often empty of people. The churches and shrines that have grown up over the centuries and the religious communities of all denominations are deserted.

Israel and Palestine are places from which many Palestinian Christians have moved, to go and live all over the world. Palestinian Christians were 30 per cent of the population of the new Israel and are now less than 1 per cent. The reasons for the diaspora are many, naturally including the political situation and the cultural, economic and educational deprivation which arise from it. Christians in the region have always struggled for an identity as Arabs, Palestinian or Israeli citizens, and also as Christians. The struggle may

---

1. *The Arab Christian*, Kenneth Cragg, Mowbray, 1992.

sometimes have been made worse for them when Messianic Jews and some Christians around the world have been seen to support the old and extreme Zionist dream of Israel as the 'promised land', an exclusive homeland for the Jewish people, thus marginalising and even excluding the Palestinian Christians and Muslims. Added to all their other worries, mainly related to the state of Israel, Christians have fears for their future in a Palestinian state where they will be a tiny minority and where their religious freedom is by no means guaranteed. When Palestinian Christians of all denominations are asked their main priorities they are quite clear. The main priority is survival. Many Christians are now saying that it is possible that they will not survive and all that will be left of Christianity in the land of its beginnings will be the holy places. This will be a very sad time not only for Christians but for people of all the faiths of the world, because though something of the spirit of the places will still be there for the pilgrims who journey to find it, the inspiration of the communities, living there day by day, year in and year out, will be lost forever.

I have visited monasteries and churches in Northern Cyprus, now a Turkish and Muslim area, where the Christian communities have gone to live in the Greek Cypriot area. In one monastery I was shown a photograph of a group of Greek Orthodox monks who were the community there before the island was divided. I could have been looking at a photograph of a hundred or more years ago and I certainly felt that I was standing in a museum of Christianity, and not in a Christian monastic church. I hope Christians all over the world will support their sisters and brothers in the Holy Land, the 'living stones', so that it never becomes a museum of lifeless stones.

The Palestinian people have, following 1947 and 1967, found themselves living in refugee camps in Lebanon, Jordan, West Bank and Gaza. They were also, by now, living all over the world, as refugees. Since the formation of Israel Jewish people have gone there from all over the world, including about 120,000 from Russia, and the state is of course heavily supported by America.

1967 saw the beginnings of a plan by Israel to control the entire region, by developing what has come to be known as a matrix of control. This plan has been intensified since 1993 and means that Israel has absolute control of key points of the matrix, so that every time the Palestinian people move they come up against yet another obstacle. When one of my colleagues joined a peace march of people of the Jewish, Muslim and Christian faiths on New Year's Eve 2001 he was also taken on a tour of the Israeli settlements around Jerusalem, the matrix of control. From one hilltop he observed:

> *Almost every hilltop has a fortress-like brand new Israeli settlement – all built contrary to the UN resolutions and to Oslo. The hillsides are decimated of the Palestinian olive groves which were the lifeblood of the villages. The Arab villages in the valleys are overlooked by the settlements, and the lands are carved up by modern highways that the Palestinians are not permitted to use . . . no compensation is offered. At present the West Bank is sealed. Villagers can barely move within a five mile radius. Access to schools, universities and hospitals is forbidden. Ambulances carrying seriously ill men, women, and children who are trying to get to hospital are stopped at road blocks and deaths of desperately ill people at road blocks are now common. Starvation is beginning to be a reality in remote villages.*[1]

The settlements and by-pass roads do not necessarily take up a lot of land. This means that the real issue today is not necessarily how much land the Palestinian people have, but

---

1. Andrew Ashdown, speaking at the Christians Aware Annual Conference in January 2002.

whether they may gain freedom within it and control over it. The Israeli government will not give up its control of the region, and its security arrangements, which include the West Bank and East Jerusalem. This of course is the main reason why the Barak offer to the Palestinians, in January 2001, of most of the West Bank, East Jerusalem and all of Gaza, was rejected by the Palestinians. They realised that having the territory was not going to give them freedom and control over that territory. Since January 2001 the violence has escalated, with suicide bombings by some young Palestinian Muslims and the cruel reprisal attacks on Palestinian areas by the Israelis. Some people now have regrets that the Barak offer was not taken up.

The first intifada, meaning uprising or resistance of the Palestinian people, began in 1987. Najwa Farah explained:

The word is deeply rooted in Arabic literature. In love poetry it speaks about that shiver that like electric currents running through the veins, causes shaking, a rise in temperature. It is the return of the soul.

Did such a shiver of passion spur the children of Palestine to rise, pick up a stone, which transformed becomes a symbol of the land.[1]

The loss of land and also of water rights was a loss of personhood for many of the Palestinian people. Land and water rights have been steadily taken away. Current policy is to pipe all the water in the West Bank away, and then to sell a tiny fraction of it back to the Palestinians. A group of Catholic sisters living in Ramallah on the West Bank wrote:

That's how we see an Arab village die, from lack of water, the underground water supply being squeezed out to the

---

1. *Colour of Courage*, Najwa Farah, Christians Aware, 1991.

depths and irrigating the conquered lands . . . in a refugee camp, they have to stand in line with their buckets for hours at the faucet because the stream of water has become so thin. A few hundred metres away, in plain sight of everyone, the water jets and sprinklers make the grass and lawns grow.[1]

The Nativity Trail is a new walk from Nazareth to Bethlehem. In April 2000 some of the Christians Aware members went on the walk and often saw wells which had been concreted down, so that the people could not get water for their animals and had to move away.

Marc Ellis, an American Jewish theologian has said that the Palestinian people are having their lives sqeezed out of them. This is a denial of Judaism, which has always had a strong sense of justice. Marc Ellis believes that for Israel to achieve its true destiny it has to take account of the Palestinian people and to do justice by them. Marc is not alone. We may be encouraged by the Jews who work for peace, for an end to the house demolitions and for justice for all in Israel and Palestine.

The aim of the first intifada was the ending of the occupation of the West Bank and Gaza and the establishment of an independent Palestine. In 1993 the Oslo Declaration was signed by Israel and the Palestinian Liberation Organisation providing for Palestinian autonomy over the Gaza strip and Jericho. This was followed by Oslo 2, which extended Palestinian authority within the West Bank. In the West Bank Area A, which is 3 per cent of the West Bank, was under Palestinian control, including seven cities. Area B, 24 per cent of the West Bank, was jointly controlled by Israel and the Palestinian Authority. Area C, 73 per cent of the West Bank, was under full Israeli control. Israel also retained control of 40 per cent of the Gaza Strip.

---

1. *Palestinian Pain and Promise*, Christians Aware, 1990.

The creation of Palestine has not solved any problems. At first Palestinians supported it, hoping it would bring a better life, but it has not. The regular sealing off of the Gaza Strip and the West Bank from East Jerusalem and from Israel in general has brought terrible hardship because Palestinians have not been able to travel to work. Family life, agriculture and trade have been disrupted. Life is severely restricted because of the use of passes and permits. The Palestinian economy has collapsed. Twenty per cent of the Palestinian people are living below the poverty line in the West Bank and Gaza. There are also great fears for the young Palestinian children who are malnourished and with little resistance to illness or to the conditions they are living in. Unemployment is among the highest in the world.

In March 1997 violence broke out again and extremists on both sides have been active. The second intifada began in September 2000, with the much publicised suicide bombings of the Palestinians most often reported through the international media. There is no security and no trust but rather a situation of war. The Palestinian areas have been bombed and invaded. It begins to be surprising that there are any people at all left in some areas. I have visited the Jerusalem Princess Basma Centre for disabled children, who report that their work has changed because the people can no longer easily bring the patients to the hospital, so that the staff members have to go out to the people. The war torn situation means that the number of patients in every department has increased dramatically.

One of my colleagues who is working in a Quaker school in Ramallah, and who is himself a Quaker and a pacifist, sent an e-mail in which he wrote:

> *There is currently no peace process. Unless there is real dialogue now, and without preconditions, there will not be an end to the armed struggle until the last Palestinian militant*

and 100s of Israelis are dead. No missile attacks, no armed incursions into Palestinian territories, no arrests or removals of militant leadership, bombardment of quasi security posts or pounding to dust already obliterated buildings will make the slightest difference, I am sorry to say, to the resolve of young men embittered by this occupation . . .[1]

He has written about the sadness he has felt on seeing the school closed, the fear he has felt on most days and nights, the optimism followed by depression, the trauma of the detonation of tank shells, the sadness of the funerals, the loneliness of the isolation and above all, the frustration as things get worse and worse. A wonderful sign of hope has been the Israeli Jew who has made many visits to Ramallah, bringing with him his van filled with food for the people.

The hope for peace and a future for all the people of Israel/Palestine can only be in the strength of the ordinary people, on all sides, to overcome the extremists on all sides. There are signs that this may be possible. There are many reports that more than a few Israeli people are beginning to criticise the Israeli Government's iron fist approach, which is provoking increasingly violent responses. There is even discussion of whether house demolitions are war crimes, especially following the demolition of homes in Gaza which left many Palestinians homeless. The Israeli peace organisations of course continue their tree planting, vigils, re-building of homes, and dismantling of blockades. The Coalition of Women for a Just Peace has been able to organise mass rallies. There was a huge rally in Tel Aviv early in 2002, organised by a whole range of peace groups. Also, and very significantly, on 26 January 2002 there was a large announcement in the *Ha'aretz* newspaper by 53 Israeli soldiers, stating, 'We hereby declare that we shall continue to serve the Israeli Defence forces in

---

1. The Quaker reports are included in a number of *Christians Aware* magazines, from 2000-2002.

any mission that serves the defence of the State of Israel. The mission of occupation and repression does not serve this goal – and we refuse to participate in it.'

The Churches have made a strong stand for peace and agreement. This has gone on over many years, but has been very strong recently. On New Year's Eve 2001, there was a march for justice and peace from Bethlehem to Jerusalem which was led by all the Church leaders in the Holy Land, together with Muslims and Jews. The aim and hope of the walk was to call for an end to the occupation of the West Bank, for Jerusalem to be opened up to all, and for people of faith to pray together. Anglican Bishop Riah was asked not to join the march by the Israeli authorities, but he remained determined. When the march began there were over 2000 Palestinians together with many Jewish people and visitors from Europe and other parts of the world. The marchers had only gone for one mile when Israeli armoured vehicles blocked the road. The church leaders walked onto the barrels of the guns and offered olive branches and asked to proceed. After lengthy negotiations the march was allowed to go on as far as the Bethlehem/Jerusalem check point, but not into Jerusalem itself. An act of worship was held at the check point by people of faith, Christians, Muslims and Jews together. Later Jews, Christians and Muslims gathered appropriately at the Pool of Bethesda and again the call for peace and healing was made.

The call for peace was also made by the Muslim, Jewish and Christian leaders in Alexandria in the New Year 2002. The leaders had the backing of the Israeli and Palestinian leaders and a permanent committee of leaders from the three faiths has been formed to pursue peace.

Issues facing all the Palestinian people, Christians and Muslims alike, are deprivation, marginalisation and lack of security. They are refugees all over the world. They have lost their land, they have very little water and they are losing their lives.

There can be no justice for the Palestinian people or for the Jewish people unless the work of Christians, Muslims and Jews for peace gathers momentum. Hope and support can only be placed behind those people who are working for peace for people of all faiths, and for a just future for all the people. We may take the side of working for justice in this conflict, but it will not help if any person or group takes the side of the Palestinian people against the Jewish people. It will not be helpful if we take the side of one group of Christians, against either the Muslim Palestinians or the Jews. This may be a temptation but the warning of Elias Chakour is clear. He does not want anyone to support the Palestinian people at the expense of the Jewish people in the Middle East. He does not wish to be separated from his Jewish neighbours, even by those who are trying to bring peace. The future of the two peoples, the three faiths, is bound up together and, in the words of Bishop Riah, 'All are loved by the one God who created them'.

The real challenge is to face the complications and struggles, knowing that God is there, at the point of meeting, in the cross. The way of meeting through the cross is inevitably painful because it refuses to recognise that there is one right way and one wrong way of going forward. The way of meeting through the cross is hard because it is the way for those who refuse to follow a straight and narrow path, which would inevitably take them away from other paths. It is for those who instead are brave enough to choose to stand at the point of meeting in the cross, the crossroads. They are peaceworkers, bridge people who recognise that most of the paths have some value. They are able to interpret people and their paths to each other and this is where hope for the future lies.

My hope is to raise awareness of this truth outside the region, supporting Palestinian and Jewish people who live in the UK, and also working for justice by visiting people in the region, as a symbol of support and care.

I am reminded of the challenge given by an Anglican peace-worker, Naim Ateek, who took his example from an American black man, Booker T. Washington, who said, of white people who had rejected him, 'I shall never permit myself to stoop so low as to hate anyone'.

The challenge in the Middle East, as always, is to work with all the people 'To act justly, to love mercy, and to walk humbly with God'.

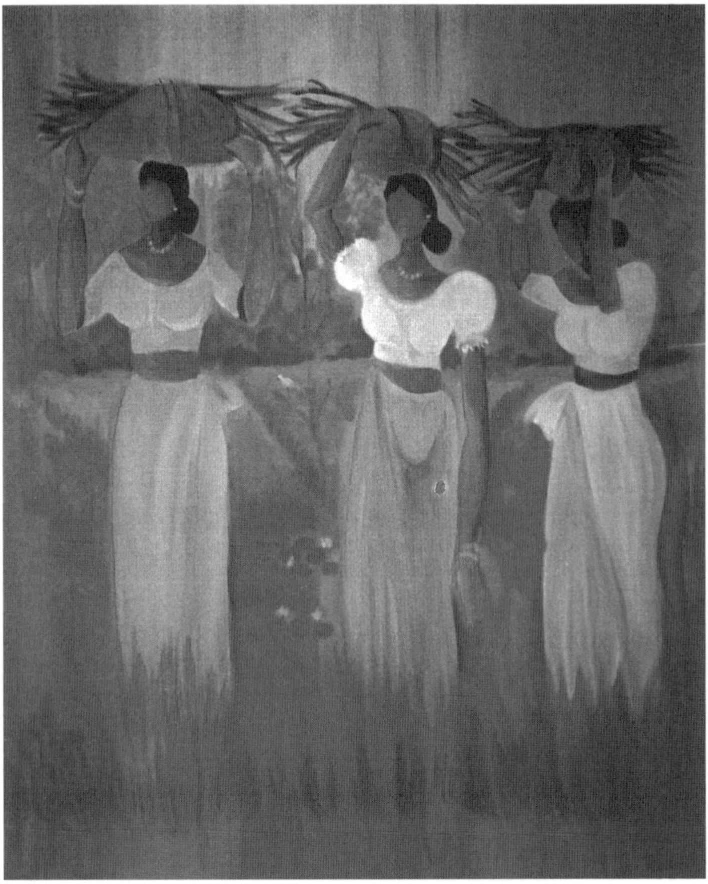

Bread in Egypt

> ... *the angel of the Lord appeareth to Joseph in a dream, saying, 'Arise, and take the young child and his mother, and flee into Egypt, and be thou there until I bring thee word: for Herod will seek the young child to destroy him'. When he arose he took the young child and his mother by night, and departed into Egypt. And was there until the death of Herod ...*
> St Matthew 2:13-15

This very short last chapter offers a glimpse of the Coptic Orthodox Church in Egypt, one of the oldest Christian communities, one whose members have, through a long and uneven history, often had to make sacrifices to keep the Church alive, to serve the beloved people and the world.

I recently met Pope Shenouda, at a gathering of Coptic Christians in Stevenage. He was there to meet members of his Coptic Orthodox Church and he had agreed to answer questions. The gathering was small, but it included people of all ages and there were many questions. Most of them were about life in the monasteries, about icons, meditation, monks and nuns. Pope Shenouda gave lengthy and interesting answers to the questions and then he gave a short talk in which he said that the monasteries were very important, but not as an end in themselves. They are there primarily to feed the spiritual needs of the people living in the villages, the community of the church.

Christian monastic life began in Egypt in the third century CE and grew rapidly. Pope Shenouda has introduced an important change of direction in monastic life, so that the monks now go out to work in the parishes much more than they did in the past. There are many young monks and the numbers, in Egypt and around the world, have grown from about 200 in 1960 to 700 in 1986, and to 1000 in 2000 CE. Most of the monks are between 25 and 40 years old.

The Coptic Orthodox Church was founded by St Mark in 42 CE. Pope Shenouda III is the 'Pope of Alexandria' today and is said to be is the most recent in an unbroken line of Patriarchs from the time of St Mark. He was born in 1923 in a village near to Assyut in Upper Egypt. When he was ordained priest it was in the monastery of Deir-es-Suriani at Wadi Natrun in 1955. He became a bishop in 1962 and head of the Church in 1971.

He is the head of the largest Christian community in the Middle East. There are more than 2 million Copts in Egypt today, and they are between 6 and 7 per cent of the population of Egypt. Some people say that the future of Christianity in the region may depend upon the Copts. There are also large Coptic communities around the world, especially in Europe, USA, Canada and Australia.

The Coptic Church values its communities of Christians enormously and the bishops, monks and married clergy work very hard for them. The Coptic Revival took place from the late 1940s and has resulted in many activities for all the age groups in the parishes.

The teaching of Pope Shenouda on the value of the Christian communities in the villages of Egypt and around the world may be understood through the Coptic Cross. The cross is made by the plaiting of pieces of leather which is symbolic of the interweaving of the cross of Christ into the world. The church cannot exist without the world, the monasteries cannot exist without the people of the world. The struggle and suffering which are part of being in the world cannot be avoided.

When I met Pope Shenouda the people at the gathering wanted him to know that they were thinking of him, in a minority situation as a Christian leader in a largely Muslim country, where from time to time there is persecution. His simple response was, 'We do not grumble when we face some of the suffering of Christ. We are happy'.

The Eucharistic bread is always round in the Coptic Eucharist. This tradition was handed down as a link between the suffering and sacrifice of Christ and the whole of creation. The round bread symbolises the universe. In the middle of the bread is a large cross, representing the Christ, with four small crosses inside it. Round the cross are 12 crosses, symbolising the 12 apostles. The 12 crosses are surrounded by the words, 'Holy, Holy, Holy, Lord God of Hosts'. All is united in worship and sacrifice. All are united with Christ and with his dedication and love.

When at the end of the service unconsecrated bread is given to the people who do not receive holy communion the link of priest and people to the wider community and world is made very clear. The link of all the people of the world to the Christ is also clear, pointing to a new life of sacrifice and joy.